# Future-Focused Wealth

# Future-Focused Wealth

## How to Build Financial Freedom at Your Own Pace

Melissa Cox CFP®

LAUREATE
LIFE PRESS

Printed in the United States of America
First Printing 2025

Publisher: Laureate Life Press, Dallas TX

ISBN: 9798218639631

*To my girls, may you embrace the strength
of running your race at your own pace.*

*To my husband, whose love and support
has helped me discover mine.*

# Table of Contents

## Introduction:
## The Importance of Future-Focused Wealth

As a Certified Financial Planner™ with over 20 years experience, I've had the pleasure—and sometimes the pain—of helping people navigate their financial lives. Trust me, I've seen it all. From those who start saving with their first paycheck, to those who finally come to me in their 50s with a sheepish look, saying, "So, uh, when do we start thinking about retirement?"

No matter their age, almost everyone I meet tells me: *I wish I had started sooner.* And you know what? I totally get it.

If I had a dollar for every time a client said, "I was too busy living in the present to think about my financial future," I'd have a lot of extra retirement savings myself. Life is busy—work, kids, bills, that Netflix series you *have* to binge. Who has time to think about retirement when you're just trying to make it through the day without burning dinner or forgetting to pick up the kids from soccer practice?

But here's the thing: Your future self is out there, waving at you frantically from 20 or 30 years down the road, hoping you don't forget about them.

And while it's true that balancing your present life with

planning for the future can feel like juggling a dozen flaming torches, the good news is that financial planning doesn't have to be overwhelming—or boring. This book, *Future-Focused Wealth*, is my way of making sure you don't end up being one of those clients who says, "I wish I'd known sooner."

We're going to talk about the important stuff—how to save, invest, plan for retirement—but we're also going to make it practical, and dare I say, enjoyable. Whether you're just starting out or playing a bit of catch-up, you'll walk away from this book with a clear plan of action that works for *you*.

### How I Became a Financial Planner by Accident

Here's something most people don't know about me: I never intended to become a financial planner. In fact, I never even took one finance class before landing in this career.

That's right—my journey into financial planning was purely accidental. And honestly, in my early days before I took my licensing exams and a cold hard look at my own personal finances, I was a lot like my clients who come in now feeling overwhelmed and confused about money. I avoided every piece of financial advice thrown my way by well-meaning relatives. I thought I had it all figured out.

Looking back, I was financially immature like a lot of hotshot young adults who think they're invincible. I wasn't thinking about long-term planning or saving for the future. I was too focused on enjoying the present and living life on my own terms. If I could go back in time and meet the younger version of myself, I probably wouldn't have given myself the job! My finances were such a mess that, frankly, I might have walked right out of my own office.

But here's the thing—your financial journey doesn't have to start out perfectly. Mine certainly didn't. That's exactly why I understand where my clients are coming from when they feel unsure or embarrassed about their finances.

I'm not ashamed to admit what a financial train wreck I was. I had learned some pretty poor money habits growing up, and I was too caught up in "looking" successful to truly allow myself to start taking control of my financial destiny.

At the age of 25, I was working two jobs to try to support a relationship in which I was the primary breadwinner in a household that clearly had Gucci taste on a Dollar Tree budget. No matter how hard I worked, the debt load never seemed to decrease. Each extra paycheck seemed to be spent on going out with friends or paying for transcontinental vacations to visit my husband's family.

When I started working in the field of finance at the age of 26, I was on the verge of a divorce and assuming a gargantuan mound of marital debt because all the credit cards were in *my* name. It didn't take long for me to feel like a fraud. If I was going to work my way up toward being an advisor, I had to get *my* financial act together. That way, I could feel honest about asking people to trust me with *their* hard-earned money. So I developed a plan, and with the support of my mom and a lot of hard work, I got my financial life under control.

The truth is, my early struggles with money made me a better financial planner in the long run. I learned through trial and error, and those experiences now allow me to guide others with empathy, understanding, and practicality. If someone like me—who avoided financial responsibility in her younger years—can learn to build wealth and make smart financial decisions, then anyone can.

MELISSA COX, CFP®

## Why Financial Planning is for Everyone

A common misconception I've encountered over the years is that financial planning is only for the wealthy—those folks with yachts, vacation homes, and trust funds. (Spoiler alert: It's not).

I've worked with clients from all financial backgrounds, and guess what? Everyone can benefit from having a plan, no matter their income or savings. It's not about how much you earn; it's about what you do with it.

Many people think they can handle it themselves—reading blogs, following "hot tips" from their favorite finance influencer, or downloading the latest budgeting app. And while those might be great tools, they often fall short of providing the personalized guidance you need. Let's be honest, trying to DIY your financial future can sometimes feel like putting together IKEA-style furniture without the instructions. You *think* you're getting it right, but somewhere along the way, a crucial piece goes missing.

Financial planning isn't about hitting arbitrary milestones or ticking boxes off a list. It's about building a road map that's specific to you—*your* goals, *your* challenges, *your* timeline. Imagine getting in a car and driving without a plan, just going wherever the road takes you. It might feel spontaneous and exciting at first, but when you arrive at what feels like your destination, you realize you can't afford the place where you've ended up.

That's what life can feel like without a financial plan—reaching a point where you've worked hard, but you're not financially prepared for the future you want. After all, it's not called the rat race for nothing.

A plan keeps you from wandering aimlessly and ensures

that you end up somewhere you actually *want* to be, both personally and financially. And the best part? It's never too early or too late to start planning.

### The Cost of Living in the Present

One of the biggest challenges we all face is balancing the now with the future. After all, life is full of items that need our immediate attention—bills, groceries, planning that family vacation you've been meaning to take. It's easy to push financial planning to the back burner. In fact, most people don't really start thinking about retirement until they're in their 40s or 50s, when the finish line suddenly feels a lot closer than they thought.

*A plan keeps you from wandering aimlessly and ensures that you end up somewhere you actually want to be, both personally and financially. And the best part? It's never too early or too late to start.*

Here's the truth: The future always shows up more quickly than you imagined. And while it's great to live in the moment (because, yes, you should enjoy life now), it's equally important to give a nod to Future You—who will really appreciate the financial planning you did back in the day. I've seen those who planned early and can cruise into retirement with peace of mind. And I've seen those who didn't. Let's just say they wish they had.

MELISSA COX, CFP®

## My Race, My Pace

I'm a big believer in the idea that everyone is on their own unique financial journey. I always tell my clients to embrace the mindset of *"my race, my pace."* It's so easy to fall into the trap of comparing yourself to others—your neighbor who seems to have it all together or your coworker who's already maxing out contributions to their retirement accounts while you're just trying to remember your online banking password.

Here's the thing: Your journey and your neighbor's are apples and oranges—two totally different paths, two completely different stories. Your life is *yours*, and it's important to focus on what's right for you, not on what anyone else is doing. Whether you're 25 or 55, what's most important is that you're taking steps, however small, toward securing your future.

It doesn't matter how you start; it only matters *that* you start. That's what this book is all about —helping you create a plan that works for *you*, with *your* goals in mind. So if you've been feeling a little behind, don't worry. There's no race to win here—only progress to be made.

### Introducing Your Training Takeaways

In *Future-Focused Wealth*, each chapter is designed to move you closer to the financial future you envision. To help you stay focused and make the most of these lessons, you'll find a section at the end of each chapter called "Training Takeaways." Think of these as your checkpoints—quick, actionable summaries that capture the chapter's key insights, guiding you to stay on course.

Just like training for a race, building a future-focused

financial plan takes consistency and commitment. Training Takeaways give you the clarity to keep moving at your own pace, reinforcing the essentials to keep your journey steady and intentional.

Whether you're glancing back for a refresher or just need a little boost to keep going, the Training Takeaways are here to support your progress, as is the glossary at the end of the book. With each chapter, you're laying a foundation for a future built with purpose, resilience, and, most importantly, at *your own pace.*

## My Goal for You

I wrote *Future-Focused Wealth* to help you build the foundation for a strong financial future—one that gives you the freedom to live your life now while still taking care of your future self. My goal is to empower you with the tools, knowledge, and confidence to take control of your finances without feeling overwhelmed or stressed out.

Over the years, I've seen so many people transform their financial lives simply by starting where they are—no matter how small their steps are. I'll be sharing real-life stories from my clients (anonymously, of course) and practical advice that you can start using right away. Whether you're just getting started or you've been in the game for a while, this book will give you the road map you need to navigate the twists and turns of your financial journey.

Let's get started on building a financial future that is designed to support you and your family through every stage of life. And remember: This is *your* race, at *your* pace. You've got this.

MELISSA COX, CFP®

# Money Concepts

# The Evolving Landscape of Finance: From Savings Accounts to a Global, Tech-Driven World

To truly grasp the importance *of Future-Focused Wealth*, it's essential to understand how the financial industry has evolved over the years. As the financial world has become more complex, so have the tools and strategies available to investors. Technology, globalization, and changing generational preferences have transformed the way we think about and manage money. To navigate this new landscape successfully, it will help you to understand where we've been, where we are, and where we're headed.

## The Shift from Simplicity to Complexity

Managing money used to be much more direct. You'd put your savings in a bank, let interest accumulate, and maybe set aside something in bonds or a pension for retirement. Your local banker was the financial expert, and options were relatively limited. Fast-forward to today, and the landscape is vastly different. The sheer range of financial products has multiplied, technology has revolutionized how we manage our finances, and the global economy presents both new opportunities and new challenges.

What's more, different generations approach money differently. Older generations tend to rely on tried-and-true methods like savings accounts and pensions. Younger generations—Millennials and Gen Z—are usually more open to riskier investments like stocks, cryptocurrencies, and using digital tools to manage their money. Understanding these generational shifts, as well as how the financial landscape has evolved, is key to successfully navigating your financial future.

For older generations, like the Silent Generation and Baby Boomers, money was typically tied up in savings accounts, bonds, or certificates of deposit (CDs). These were seen as secure, long-term investments that provided safety and stability. People relied on their local banks to safeguard their money and give them interest in return. At the time, this was enough to build a secure financial future.

But today, those traditional methods have their limitations. Interest rates are historically low, meaning that savings accounts and bonds no longer provide the same kind of growth they once did. While they still offer stability, they're not always enough to keep up with inflation or provide the growth needed to build long-term wealth.

### The Rise of Stock Market Investing

Things began to shift with the Baby Boomer generation as traditional retirement pension plans—which had guaranteed a set income for life after retirement—started to be phased out. This meant that fewer employers offered pensions as part of their benefits. Many employers began to replace them with

401(k) plans instead. Unlike pensions, which are managed entirely by employers, 401(k) plans require individuals to contribute a portion of their salary and often make decisions about how that money is invested. This shift placed

more responsibility on individuals to take an active role in planning for their retirement.

Around this time, the stock market also saw significant growth, partly fueled by the introduction of 401(k) accounts—first established in 1978—and the increasing popularity of mutual funds. While mutual funds have been around longer than 401(k) accounts, they became much more accessible in the 1980s. A 401(k) allows employees to invest a portion of their paycheck in various assets, such as stocks and bonds, often with some matching contribution from their employer. Mutual funds, on the other hand, pool money from multiple investors to invest in a diversified portfolio of stocks, bonds, or other securities.

Together, these accounts offered people a way to grow their money more substantially over time compared to traditional savings accounts or bonds, which typically provide lower, fixed returns.

Generation X followed suit, embracing mutual funds and individual stock trading as a means of building wealth. For this generation, investing in the stock market became a key tool in securing financial stability for the future.

MELISSA COX, CFP®

Then came the Millennials and Gen Z, who have taken stock-market investing to the next level with the rise of digital platforms and apps. Companies like Robinhood and Acorns made it easier than ever for anyone to start investing with just a few dollars, democratizing access to the stock market. The shift from simply saving to actively investing became more pronounced as younger generations realized that to build wealth, they needed to grow their money—not just safeguard it.

## New Financial Products and a Global Economy: A World of Choices for Modern Generations

As financial products have evolved, people now have more options than ever. For Millennials and Gen Z, Exchange-Traded Funds (ETFs) have become a popular choice. ETFs offer the diversification of mutual funds but with lower fees and the ability to trade like stocks. This flexibility and low cost have made them an attractive option for younger generations looking for long-term growth.

At the same time, global ETFs and international markets are opening up new ways to diversify beyond the U.S. market, which resonates with younger generations who have grown up in a globally connected world.

**Exchange-Traded Funds (ETF)**

A bundle of securities that trades on an exchange like a stock.

This shift toward a global approach also includes foreign exchange (Forex) investments and digital currencies that operate on an international scale. For instance, cryptocurrencies like Bitcoin and Ethereum offer a decentralized form of currency that isn't tied to any one country, appealing to younger investors looking for alternatives to traditional financial

> **Cryptocurrency**
>
> A digital currency that operates on blockchain technology, such as Bitcoin or Ethereum, known for its decentralized nature and price volatility.

systems. Though highly volatile, these digital assets provide the allure of decentralization and high-growth potential, especially for those looking to diversify in nontraditional ways.

In addition, robo-advisors like Betterment and Wealthfront have made investing even more accessible. These platforms use algorithms to automatically invest money based on your goals and risk tolerance, making investing simpler and more hands-off. The appeal for younger generations is clear: low fees, easy access, and minimal effort.

Similarly, real estate crowdfunding platforms such as Fundrise have also emerged, allowing people to invest in real estate with smaller amounts of capital. This is another area where traditional barriers to entry have been lowered, creating new ways for people to diversify their investments.

However, while the global economy presents many new opportunities, it also comes with unique risks. Currency fluctuations, geopolitical instability, and global market volatility are all factors to consider when investing internationally.

With careful planning and the right strategy, younger generations can leverage these diverse financial products

MELISSA COX, CFP®

and global markets to build robust, diversified portfolios that reflect their unique perspectives and ambitions.

## The Evolution of Financial Professionals: From Bankers to Family Offices

The role of financial professionals has changed significantly over the years, shaped by generational needs and shifts in the financial landscape.

For the Silent Generation and early Baby Boomers, local bankers were the go-to financial experts. They provided safe, stable options like savings accounts, bonds, and loans. Their role was largely to safeguard people's money rather than to help them grow it.

As the Baby Boomers began to invest in the stock market, the commission-based financial advisor became more common. These advisors helped sell financial products like mutual funds and insurance policies, often earning commissions on the products they sold. While these advisors helped people grow their money, they were often sales-driven, which could lead to conflicts of interest.

Generation X and Millennials have shifted toward comprehensive financial planners who focus on more holistic financial strategies. Instead of just selling products, these professionals help clients with everything from budgeting to retirement planning, investments, taxes, and estate planning. This comprehensive approach, often working with a Certified Financial Planner™ (CFP®) reflects the increasing complexity of the financial world. The CFP® designation is one of the most respected credentials in the financial industry, requiring rigorous education, hands-on experience, and a commitment to ethical standards. Earning the CFP® involves completing coursework in financial planning, passing a comprehensive exam, and gaining real-world experience, all of which prepare CFP® professionals to guide clients through every aspect of their financial lives.

For high-net-worth individuals and families, the family office model has emerged as a way to provide fully integrated financial management. These offices offer services beyond investments, including tax strategy, philanthropy, and estate planning. While family offices cater to the wealthy, Millennials and Gen Z are using digital tools to access similar comprehensive financial management, and there is a shift in comprehensive financial planning firms to provide the same access to clients.

### Living Longer, Needing More in Retirement

One of the most significant changes in recent years is the increase in life expectancy. Maybe it's modern medicine, or maybe people are just hanging around a little longer hoping to see the Chicago Cubs win another World Series. Whatever the reason, people are living longer than ever, and that means they need to plan for longer retirements. With the average life expectancy rising significantly, retirees now find themselves needing more money to cover those extra years of living expenses and healthcare costs—because let's face it, those Cubs tickets aren't getting any cheaper!

In the past, it was assumed that you would need about 70% of your annual pre-retirement salary each year in retirement to maintain a comfortable lifestyle. For example, if you earned $100,000 per year before retiring, the idea was that

MELISSA COX, CFP®

you'd need around $70,000 per year in retirement to cover your expenses. This estimate took into account that certain costs, like commuting or saving for retirement, would likely decrease in retirement.

However, with people living longer, spending more, and the costs of healthcare and living rising, that percentage has increased. Experts now recommend aiming for a higher percentage of 80-100% of your pre-retirement income to ensure you can maintain your lifestyle throughout retirement.

Additionally, rising healthcare costs are one of the largest factors contributing to the increased need for retirement savings. As people live longer, they face more significant medical expenses, and it's crucial to account for this in retirement planning. Planning for a longer retirement and saving more aggressively are now essential to ensuring financial security in the later stages of life.

## Navigating the Changing Financial Landscape

With all these changes in the financial landscape, how do you navigate it successfully?

The key is finding the right balance between traditional, stable financial products and the newer, riskier options available today. Diversification is critical, no matter your age or financial background. While older generations may prefer the safety of savings accounts and bonds, and younger generations may prefer to explore riskier investments like stocks and cryptocurrencies, everyone needs a well-rounded plan that takes both *stability* and *growth* into account.

It's also important to stay informed. The financial world is evolving rapidly, and it's easy to fall behind. Whether you're managing your own investments or working with a financial planner, keeping up with the latest trends and products is crucial to making smart financial decisions.

## Generational Perspectives and the Future of Finance

Every generation's approach to money has been influenced by the economic conditions they experienced. For instance, the oldest generation, who lived through or grew up hearing about the Great Depression, often prioritize safety and stability in their financial choices. This generation tends to favor traditional tools like savings accounts, bonds, and pensions, seeking security in financial products that minimize risk.

*The CFP® designation is one of the most respected credentials in the financial industry, requiring rigorous education, hands-on experience, and a commitment to ethical standards.*

Younger generations embrace technology-driven solutions and are more willing to take on higher risks. The future of finance will likely merge these perspectives, blending the reliability of traditional savings with the dynamic opportunities of a global, tech-centered economy.

Financial professionals now act more like guides, helping clients navigate a complex world of financial products, technology, and global markets. Whether you're a Baby Boomer planning for retirement or a Millennial looking to grow your investments, having a plan that can adapt to these changes is key to long-term success.

*Training Takeaway:*
*Navigating the Changing Financial Landscape*

The financial world has transformed dramatically over the years, and understanding its evolution is essential to creating a successful plan for the future. From traditional savings accounts to the rise of stock-market investing, innovative digital tools, and the globalization of finance, today's investors face more choices—and challenges—than ever before.

To thrive in this dynamic environment, it's crucial to balance the stability of tried-and-true methods with the opportunities of modern strategies. Whether it's leveraging new financial products like ETFs and robo-advisors or planning for longer retirements, staying informed and adaptable will ensure you're ready for whatever the future holds. After all, successful financial planning is about blending the wisdom of the past with the possibilities of tomorrow.

## Understanding the Concept of Money

Let's be honest—we all think we understand money because we use it every day. But when you really dig into what it means and how it works, it gets a little more complicated. Think of it like a smartphone—you might know how to use it for calls and apps, but most of us have no clue how it actually works. And that's okay! When it comes to money, the basics are simple, but the deeper understanding is where things get interesting—and important.

In this chapter, we're going to break down what money really is, why it matters, and how understanding it can change the way you handle your finances. Spoiler alert: It's not just about cash, cards, or even cryptocurrencies. And yes, we'll answer the age-old question: *Can money really buy happiness?* Short answer: Not exactly, but it sure can help if you know how to manage it.

### The Evolution of Money

Once upon a time, money didn't exist. People traded stuff—like cows for grain or pottery for fish. Eventually, someone

MELISSA COX, CFP®

*Here's one of the biggest misconceptions about money: the idea that people from wealthy families automatically understand how money works, and people from less affluent backgrounds don't. Not true.*

figured out it would be easier to carry coins in your pocket than a cow. And voilà, money as we know it was born. Fast forward to today, and we've gone from coins and bills to plastic and now digital currencies.

While the way we use money has evolved, our understanding of its value hasn't always kept up. Some people think having a lot of money is the ultimate goal (cue images of Scrooge McDuck diving into his pile of gold coins), while others see it as something mysterious and out of reach. The truth? Money is a tool—a pretty useful one—but it's not the end-all-be-all. It's what you do with it that counts.

We've all heard the saying "money is the root of all evil." But in reality, money is neutral. It's like a hammer—you can use it to build a house, or you can accidentally whack your thumb with it. The hammer doesn't care. The same goes for money. It's not inherently good or bad, but how you use it makes all the difference.

Some people think money will solve all their problems. It won't. Others find it overwhelming and avoid thinking about it entirely--also not a great idea. The truth is somewhere in the middle. Money can't fix everything, but it can help if you learn to manage it well. The trick is to see it not as a magical solution but as a resource to help you build the life you want.

Here's one of the biggest misconceptions about money: the idea that people from wealthy families automatically understand how money works, and people from less affluent backgrounds don't. Not true. Financial literacy is not tied to your background—it's tied to education and experience. I've seen clients who grew up with wealth and had no idea how to manage it. On the flip side, I've worked with people who came from modest beginnings but understood the value of every dollar they earned.

The truth is, money doesn't come with an instruction manual, no matter where you're from. That's why it's so important to learn the basics of managing money—setting financial priorities, distinguishing between needs and wants, and developing solid financial habits.

Regardless of your background, you have the power to become financially literate and take control of your money.

### The Real Value of Money: Needs vs. Wants

One of the biggest struggles with money is figuring out the difference between needs and wants. Let's be real—sometimes that shiny new gadget or fancy vacation feels like a need, but nine times out of ten, it's actually a want. And that's fine, as long as you know how to prioritize.

Needs are the essentials: housing, food, healthcare, and the basics that keep you alive and well. Wants? Well, they're the fun stuff. Whether it's that designer handbag, a brand-new phone, or treating yourself to that artisanal chocolate you can't pronounce (we've all been there)—those are extras. The key

MELISSA COX, CFP®

is making sure your needs are met before you indulge in the wants.

Understanding this balance is critical when it comes to managing money. Sure, splurging on something nice once in a while is great, but you don't want to get into a situation where your "want" spending leaves you short on covering your "needs." (Hint: That's where budgets come in handy—but don't worry, I promise we'll get to that.)

### Money Mindsets: Abundance vs. Scarcity

Here's the thing: How you *think* about money is just as important as how much of it you have.

If you have a scarcity mindset, where you're always worried there's never enough, it can feel like you're constantly on edge, no matter how much you earn. On the flip side, having an abundance mindset, where you recognize money as a tool that brings opportunities, can help you make better financial decisions and feel more in control.

I've worked with clients who grew up without much, and even after they started earning more, they still had a scarcity mindset, always feeling like they were just one step away from financial disaster. I've also seen people with modest incomes who felt financially secure because they knew how to balance their money well. It's not about how *much* you have—it's about how you think about it and how you manage it.

At the end of the day, money is just a tool. It's not something to obsess over, but it's also not something to ignore. It's there to help you meet your needs, achieve your goals, and yes, indulge in the occasional treat. The key is to know how to manage it wisely.

Money won't solve all your problems, but it can definitely make life easier if you understand its value and how to make it work for you. Whether you're managing a little or a lot, remember that it's not about how much money you have; rather, it's about how well you use it to create the life you want. And yes, that life can include the occasional splurge on avocado toast—as long as you're keeping the big picture in mind.

### Training Takeaway: Mastering Money's True Purpose

Money isn't just paper, plastic, or digital currency—it's a tool. Like any tool, its value lies in how you use it. From balancing needs and wants to overcoming scarcity mindsets, understanding the true nature of money can empower you to make better financial decisions.

Whether your financial journey started with privilege or perseverance, remember that financial literacy is learned, not inherited. Prioritize building your knowledge, mastering the basics, and viewing money as a resource to craft the life you want. It's not about how much you have—it's about how wisely you use what you have.

A solid foundation is the key to stability in any structure, and your financial life is no different. The strength of that foundation—whether it's built on savings, investments, or simply a plan—determines how well you can weather the storms that inevitably come.

Just like the earth shifts beneath a house, life brings changes that can shake the very ground beneath your financial foundation. Over time, the terrain might not be as stable as it once was. But the stronger the base, the better equipped you are to handle whatever comes your way.

MELISSA COX, CFP®

# 3

## Laying the Foundation
## for Your Personalized Financial Future

If there's one phrase I hear more than any other, it's this: *I wish I had started sooner.* Whether it's saving, investing, or even just having a plan, most people feel like they're behind. And honestly, I get it. Life comes at you fast—there's work, kids, bills, and about a million other things demanding your attention.

It's no wonder that long-term financial planning often takes a back seat to the here and now. But that's why I'm here—to help you balance both.

### Building a Healthy Relationship with Money

Let's be real: Talking about money can be awkward. It's right up there with talking about politics at the dinner table or trying to explain why you haven't been to the gym since January (no judgment). But if you want to build a solid financial future, you need to start by having honest conversations about money—both with yourself and, if applicable, with your partner and family.

Over the years, I've found that the clients who make the most progress are the ones who aren't afraid to tackle their financial situation head-on, no matter how messy it might seem at first. They're the ones who recognize that even small, consistent steps—like setting up automatic savings or trimming down unnecessary expenses—can add up to big changes over time.

*This is a lesson worth hearing over and over, because it's essential to financial success: There's no one-size-fits-all path to financial well-being.*

Think of it like planting a garden. You might not see much growth at first, but give it time, and soon you'll have something you can be proud of. But skip the maintenance, and that garden could quickly turn into either a jungle of weeds or a barren desert.

## The Importance of Starting Early

If there's one message I hope to get across in this book, it's this: *Start as early as you can.* Now, if you're reading this and thinking, "But I'm already in my 40s; isn't it too late for me?" Don't worry, you're not alone. But here's the good news: There's no such thing as "too late" when it comes to your financial health. Starting early gives you the added benefit of compound growth, but that doesn't mean you're out of options if you start later.

MELISSA COX, CFP®

Here's a fun fact: Compound growth is like a snowball rolling down a hill. The earlier you start rolling that snowball, the bigger it gets as it collects more snow. And while we can't control the size of the hill (or the snowball), we *can* control when we start pushing. Even if you're pushing a little later in life, you can still make meaningful progress.

In fact, some of my clients who start in their 40s or 50s end up more focused and determined than those who started in their 20s. They know they need to make up for lost time, and they're willing to do the work. So if you're sitting there thinking you've missed your chance, stop worrying. We've got this.

### The Cost of Living ONLY in the Present

Now, let's talk about the flip side: *living only in the present*. It's something I touched on briefly, but like a dripping faucet, this is a point worth repeating until it really sinks in: Living in the present is essential—but so is preparing for the future. We all have to do it. When it comes to your finances, it's all about finding a balance between enjoying today and planning for tomorrow; it's easier said than done, I know.

Many of my clients, especially those in their 40s and 50s, tell me stories about how they spent money on things that seemed important at the time—fancy dinners, the latest gadgets, vacations—only to realize later that they hadn't set anything aside for their long-term goals. And let's be clear: It's not that they were wrong to enjoy life. After all, what's the point of financial success if you're not enjoying the journey? But as we've said, the trick is learning how to enjoy *both* the present and the future.

## My Race, My Pace

In a world where everyone's financial journey seems to be on display, it's easy to fall into the trap of comparing yourself to others.

Maybe a friend bought a house at 30, or your sibling seems to have their retirement contributions fully maxed out, and suddenly it feels like you're falling behind. But here's the reality: Your financial journey is unique, and what works for someone else might not be the right fit for you.

If this sounds a bit repetitive, that's intentional—research shows it takes hearing a lesson around seven times before it really sinks in. And this is a lesson worth hearing over and over, because it's essential to financial success: There's no one-size-fits-all path to financial well-being.

Progress doesn't have to mean hitting every traditional milestone by a certain age; it means moving toward a life that's sustainable for you at a pace that keeps you steady and grounded. Take a deep breath and remember—there's no finish line you need to rush across. You're setting the pace, so focus on what aligns with your goals, your values, and your vision for the future.

## Balancing Today and Tomorrow

Finding that balance between living for today and planning for tomorrow is key. It can be tricky, but that's why consistency is your greatest tool. You don't have to make drastic changes or big sacrifices; it's the small, intentional steps that make a lasting impact. Whether it's setting up an automatic transfer to your savings account or investing a manageable portion of your income, these small actions add up over time.

Think of your financial journey as a road trip. You're enjoying the ride, but you're also keeping an eye on the fuel gauge to ensure you reach your destination. You don't have to map out every detail, but you do need to keep an eye on the big picture. And just like a road trip, it's okay to take it slowly, stop when you need to, and adjust your route as you go. Financial success is built over time—at *your* pace, in *your* way.

At the end of the day, financial planning isn't just about numbers, investments, or retirement accounts; it's about peace of mind. It's about knowing that whatever life throws your way, you've got a plan in place.

In this moment, focus on the building blocks that will bring you closer to your goals—setting clear intentions, creating a budget that fits your life, managing debt in a way that doesn't feel overwhelming. It's about making decisions that work for you right now. As you continue to build financial skills, you'll naturally delve into more complex topics like investing and retirement planning, and you'll navigate the emotional side of money—because let's face it, money isn't just about dollars and cents.

### *Training Takeaway: Building Your Financial Foundation— Your Race, Your Pace*

Creating a strong financial foundation is about more than just numbers; it's about consistency, balance, and taking intentional steps toward your goals. Whether you're starting in your 20s, 40s, or beyond, remember: It's your race, and it's at your pace.

Focus on small, steady actions like budgeting, saving, and learning to balance today's joys with tomorrow's security. Don't get distracted by comparisons or milestones that don't align with your journey. Progress is personal, and success comes from building a life that works for you—not anyone else.

Keep your eyes on the big picture, enjoy the ride, and take pride in every step forward. Your financial future is built over time, and with a solid foundation, you can move forward with confidence and peace of mind.

# Creating and Organizing
## Your Personal Financial Binder

When it comes to managing your finances, organization is key—whether you're a pro at spreadsheets or a lover of color-coded binders. A well-organized financial binder isn't just for show; it can make a huge difference in how you manage your money and provide peace of mind for your family. Think of it as your financial "in case of emergency" kit—everything neatly arranged in one place so that your loved ones can easily access it if they need to.

This chapter will walk you through how to create and organize your personal financial binder, step by step. By the end of this process, you'll feel empowered, in control, and ready to tackle whatever financial curveballs life throws at you.

## Why Organizing Your Financial Information Matters

Having all your financial information in one place isn't just about feeling like a financial superhero, though that's a nice bonus. It's about being prepared for the unexpected.

Whether it's an emergency, a family crisis, or simply the need to update your financial plan, knowing where everything is can save you and your loved ones a lot of headaches.

I've seen too many families scramble because they didn't know where the important documents were or didn't have access to key financial information. Trust me, the last thing you want is your family trying to piece together your financial life during a crisis.

You might be someone who prefers to keep everything online—after all, apps and cloud storage are incredibly convenient. However, your family might not be as comfortable navigating your digital setup.

A physical binder provides a backup in case they need easy access or if there's an issue with your online accounts (hello, password lockouts). Plus, you never know when a technical glitch or forgotten password might lock you out of your own digital fortress.

A binder is like the analog insurance policy you didn't know you needed.

### Getting Started: Gather Your Supplies (and Pick Your Favorite Binder)

Before you start wrangling documents, you'll need to gather some basic supplies. And yes, this is your permission to head to your favorite office supply store and pick out the biggest, most colorful binder you can find. You want something sturdy. Think of it as the "ultimate, indestructible binder" that can hold everything you need to safeguard your financial future. This isn't your average folder; it's the hefty size—because this binder is going to hold *everything*. You'll need:

- A 3-ring binder (the bigger, the better)
- 15 divider tabs (or more)

- Sheet protectors (lots of them)
- A paper notebook (for manually tracking account details and goals)

Pro tip: Choose a binder in a color that makes you happy. Organizing your finances doesn't have to be boring, and a neon pink or vibrant blue binder can give you that extra boost of motivation to get things done.

### Step 1: Create Your Dividers

Your binder will be divided into different sections based on the key areas of your financial life. Here are the main categories I recommend, though feel free to customize based on your needs:

- Financial Goals
- Master Account and Professional Contact List (for easy reference)
- Estate Planning Documents
- Sources of Income
- Credit Reports
- Bank Accounts
- Savings Accounts
- Investment Accounts
- Life Insurance Policies
- Other Insurance Policies
- Real Estate or Rental Information
- Service Providers (Monthly/Annual Bills)
- Credit Cards
- Loans (Car, Student, Personal)
- Tax Returns

Each of these tabs will house relevant documents, making it easy to find everything when you need it. If you're missing something (like an estate plan), this is a good time to make a note to get that taken care of.

### Step 2: Start Filling in the Binder

Now that your binder is set up, it's time to start gathering and organizing your documents. You're going to place each document behind the appropriate divider tab. Here's a breakdown of what you should include in each section:

- **Financial Goals**. Start by jotting down your short, medium, and long-term goals. These might change over time, so don't worry about getting them perfect right now. Short-term goals might include paying off debt or building an emergency fund, while long-term goals could be retirement or saving for a major purchase.

- **Master Account and Contact List.** Use this section to keep a master list of all your accounts—bank accounts, investment accounts, insurance policies, etc. Include contact information for each account, as well as your online login details. This is especially important in case a family member needs to access your accounts on your behalf.

- **Estate Planning Documents**. Place copies of your estate planning documents here, including your will, trusts, and powers of attorney. Make sure to note where the originals are stored and who else has copies. For example, "Original copy in the safe and with my sister." Originals should be kept in a fireproof safe, not a bank vault, since banks may lock down vaults upon your death, making access difficult. Copies of other important legal documents, like birth or death certificates, marriage/divorce records, passports/ IDs, and funeral or burial plans, should also be stored here.

- **Sources of Income.** Include your most recent pay stubs, W-2s, Social Security statements, or pension information. This section helps you keep track of where your money is coming from and can be useful when updating your financial plan or filing taxes.

- **Credit Reports.** Pull a credit report from each of the three major reporting agencies (Equifax, Experian, and TransUnion). It's a good idea to check these reports regularly for accuracy and to monitor for any signs of fraud.

- **Bank Accounts.** Put copies of your bank account statements in this section. This is also a great place to make note of any automatic payments you have set up.

- **Savings Accounts.** Place your savings account statements here. It's important to keep track of your savings so you can monitor your progress toward building an emergency fund or reaching other financial goals.

- **Investment Accounts.** Include year-end statements for all investment accounts, whether they're retirement accounts (like a 401(k) or IRA) or taxable investment accounts. If you have an employer-sponsored retirement plan, this is a good place to keep a copy of the plan summary.

- **Life Insurance Policies.** Add your life insurance policy information, along with any recent illustrations or reports your insurance broker has provided. Understanding the details of your policy can help you and your loved ones be prepared for the future.

- **Other Insurance Policies.** This tab can house everything from homeowner's or renter's insurance, to auto insurance and disability policies. If you have insurance for your jewelry, pets, or anything else, put those policies here as well.

- **Real Estate or Rental Information**. Include mortgage statements, property tax assessments, rental agreements, or any information related to rental properties you own. If you're a real estate investor, be sure to include property management contracts here as well.

- **Service Providers (Monthly/Annual Bills)**. Gather your monthly bills for things like utilities, cell phones, and internet service. This helps you keep track of regular expenses and spot any unexpected increases.

- **Credit Cards**. Put copies of your latest credit card statements here. If you have multiple cards, give each one its own section. This is also where you'll want to include any annual summaries provided by your credit card companies.

- **Loans**. This is where you'll keep information about any car loans, student loans, or personal loans. Make sure to include details like balances, interest rates, and payment schedules.

- **Tax Returns**. Place copies of your last two or three years of tax returns here. This can help you keep track of your financial history and is useful when planning for future tax filings.

- **Other Optional Tabs.** The sky's the limit with this binder. Some of my clients have also included passwords or password recovery info, church information, and military or discharge information.

### Step 3: Take a Break (You've Earned It!)

Once you've gathered all your documents and organized

MELISSA COX, CFP®

them into your binder, take a well-deserved break. This is no small task, especially if it's your first time pulling everything together. Remember, this binder isn't just for you—it's a gift to your future self and your family, making it easier for everyone to navigate your finances when the time comes.

For some, putting this binder together can stir up a lot of emotions, especially if you've been avoiding your finances or dealing with financial stress. It's normal to feel anxious or overwhelmed. But remember, this is a step toward taking control of your financial future. Be patient with yourself. You're not expected to have all the answers immediately— just getting organized is a huge win.

### How Long Should You Keep Your Records?

Once you've organized your financial binder, it's important to know how long to keep certain documents. After all, nobody wants their binder bursting at the seams with paperwork from 20 years ago! Here's a quick guide to help you decide what needs to stay and what can go.

- **Tax Documents**: 7 years. The IRS recommends keeping tax returns and supporting documents for at least seven years. This includes W-2s, 1099s, and any receipts or documentation for deductions. If you're ever audited, you'll be grateful you held onto these.
- **Bank Statements**: 1-7 years. Generally, bank statements can be kept for a year unless they are tied to your tax returns, in which case, hold them for seven years. Many banks provide online access to older statements, so this could also save some binder space. (My preference: Only keep the end-of-the-year statement and Annual

Summary, unless you do not have online access.)

- **Loan Documents**: Until the loan is paid off. For car loans, mortgages, and other types of debt, keep records until the loan is fully paid off and the title or deed is clear. Once settled, it's safe to shred them, but keep proof of payment for a few extra years just in case.
- **Insurance Policies**: Until renewed. Keep copies of your current insurance policies (home, auto, life, etc.) until they're renewed. Once a new policy is issued, you can shred the old one—just make sure you have documentation of any claims made.
- **Estate Documents**: Forever. Estate planning documents such as your will, powers of attorney, and trust agreements should always be kept in your binder. Make sure a trusted family member knows where the originals are kept and has access in case of an emergency.

By following these guidelines, you can ensure your binder stays organized and clutter-free. Plus, you'll have peace of mind knowing that you've kept everything for the right amount of time.

## When to Have the "Binder" Discussion

Now, let's talk about one of the most important conversations you'll ever have about your finances: the "binder" discussion. It might not sound like the most exciting family chat, but it's crucial for keeping everyone in the loop about financial decisions, emergency plans, and estate matters.

So, when's the right time to bring this up?

The answer is sooner rather than later—don't wait for someone to be diagnosed with a terminal illness or placed

MELISSA COX, CFP®

in hospice or for chaos to strike. It's best to hash things out when everyone's clear-headed, calm, and not in the middle of a family crisis (or a heated game of Monopoly). Oh, and you definitely don't want it to be misidentified as some kind of intervention! Future-you will thank present-you for getting this done while things are still smooth sailing.

## How to Bring It Up

Schedule a specific time to talk about it, preferably when everyone's available and in a comfortable, non-stressful environment. No one wants to discuss estate plans during Thanksgiving dinner or when kids are running around.

Lead with the why. Open with the practical stuff. You're not being grim, just realistic! We all know there is no cure for death, and nature is going to win 100% of the time. Explain that having this binder organized is like creating a family safety net—so no one's left scrambling if something happens. It's not about expecting the worst; it's about making sure everyone knows what to do, who to call, and where to find those all-important documents.

Some family members may be hesitant or even resistant to the discussion. They might find it uncomfortable or overwhelming. Let them know this is just about preparation, and it can help avoid bigger problems down the road. Ease them into the conversation by focusing on the practical aspects rather than the emotional weight of the topic. And don't be surprised if you get a range of reactions. Some family members might be relieved you're taking the initiative (bonus points for being the responsible one), while others might act like you're trying to read them your will right then and there.

Stay calm and persistent, and remind them that getting all the financial ducks in a row now will save everyone from future stress—and protect the family's financial security. But it's also important to emphasize that the inheritance you hope to leave them *cannot* be their retirement plan. Let them know they will need to plan for their own financial future, but you do hope any inheritance will help.

### Training Takeaway: Organization as Empowerment

Creating a personal financial binder might sound old school, but it's one of the most empowering things you can do for yourself and your family. Not only will it help you feel more in control of your finances, but it will also provide a road map for your loved ones in case they ever need to step in.

So grab that neon binder, organize your documents, and give yourself a pat on the back. You've just taken a huge step toward financial empowerment.

## Building a Budget: Finding What Works for You

Budgeting might seem simple—and, to some extent, it is. After all, a budget is just a way to track your income and expenses, right? But here's the thing: Budgets are like diets. Sure, the basic concept is straightforward, but anyone who's ever tried a fad diet knows that being too aggressive can leave you feeling frustrated and ready to throw in the towel. It's the same with budgeting. You need to find the method that works for you and your lifestyle; otherwise, you risk derailing your best efforts before you even get started.

### Budgets Options

Ah, budgeting. It's not exactly the most exciting part of personal finance, but it's hands down one of the most important. Think of your budget as the foundation of your financial house—if it's shaky, everything else is going to wobble. But if it's solid, you can build on it with confidence.

Now, I know what you're thinking: *Do I really need a budget?* Yes, you really do. I can't tell you how many clients I've worked with who thought they were doing fine without one, only to realize that their money was disappearing faster than they could figure out why. A budget gives you a road map. It shows you exactly where your money is going and helps you prioritize what matters most.

*A budget gives you a roadmap. When you budget intentionally, you'll find that you actually have more control and more freedom with your money— not less.*

Creating a budget doesn't have to be painful, and it doesn't mean you have to cut out all the fun stuff in life. It's about balance. You can absolutely still enjoy your Friday night takeout or your morning coffee— just make sure those things are part of the plan. When you budget intentionally, you'll find that you actually have *more* control and *more* freedom with your money, not less.

Just like there are countless diets promising to be the best way to shed pounds, there are plenty of budgeting methods that claim to be the best for managing your money. But here's the reality: There's no one-size-fits-all solution.

Whether you're a DINK (Dual Income, No Kids) trying to maximize your disposable income, a HENRY (High Earner, Not Rich Yet) working to balance your current lifestyle with future financial goals, a young family, someone just learning the basics, or someone trying to navigate planning for retirement, *finding the right budgeting method is key.*

The key is to find the method that aligns with your goals, your spending habits, and—most importantly—your personality. No matter where you are on your financial journey, there's a budgeting style that can fit your needs and help you reach your goals. Now we'll explore a few popular approaches.

## The 50/30/20 Budget

This is a great starting point for anyone new to budgeting because it's simple yet effective. The 50/30/20 rule divides your income into three categories:

- 50% for needs (housing, groceries, utilities)
- 30% for wants (dining out, entertainment, shopping)
- 20% for savings and debt repayment.

It's a flexible approach that allows you to prioritize saving and paying off debt while still leaving room for some fun. Think of it as a balanced diet for your finances—you're getting what you need while also enjoying a few treats along the way.

## Zero-Based Budget

This method is like a strict meal plan—you account for every dollar. With a zero-based budget, you assign every dollar of income to a specific category, whether it's bills, savings, or discretionary spending. The goal? Your income minus your expenses should equal zero at the end of the month.

This method works well for people who like structure and want to ensure no dollar is unaccounted for. But be warned—it can feel a bit restrictive if you're not naturally detail-oriented.

## Pay Yourself First

If the idea of tracking every dollar makes you break out in a sweat, this method is more relaxed. With the pay-yourself-first method, you focus on saving and investing right off the top of your income—typically 15-20%—then live off the rest.

The idea is to prioritize your savings goals and avoid the temptation to spend money just because it's available. This method works well if you're disciplined about saving but want more flexibility in how you spend the rest of your money.

## The FIRE Budget (Financial Independence, Retire Early)

If you've ever dreamed of retiring decades earlier than the norm, the FIRE movement might be right up your alley. FIRE is all about saving and investing aggressively in your 20s and 30s with the goal of reaching financial independence by your 40s or even earlier.

The key is to minimize expenses as much as possible, maximize savings, and invest the difference to create a portfolio that can support you for the rest of your life. FIRE also comes in a few flavors:

- Lean FIRE: For those who live on a very minimalist budget in retirement.
- Fat FIRE: For those who want more flexibility and a higher standard of living when they retire.
- Barista FIRE: A mix of semi-retirement where you cover some expenses with part-time work while drawing on savings and investments.

## Build Your Budget Step 1:
## Know Your Income—All of It

Before you even think about building a budget, you need to take a deep dive into your income. Sounds straightforward, right? Well, there's more to it than just glancing at your paycheck. It's about understanding all sources of income, being crystal clear on your gross income, and knowing exactly what your taxable rate is.

It's important to know both your gross income (the total amount you earn before any deductions) and your net income (what's left after taxes, retirement contributions, and other deductions). Most people focus only on their take-home pay, but knowing your gross income helps you see the full picture, including how much of your hard-earned money is going to taxes, healthcare, and other contributions.

### Gross Income

The total amount you earn before any deductions are taken out.

### Net Income

Your gross income minus taxes, retirement contributions, healthcare costs, and any other automatic contributions.

Examining your paycheck is crucial because it shows exactly how much you're paying for things like healthcare and retirement contributions. For example, if you're contributing to a 401(k), that money is coming out pre-tax, which can lower your taxable income and potentially reduce how much you owe come tax time. Understanding how these deductions affect your overall income gives you more control over your financial planning.

If you have more than one source of income (side gigs, rental income, or investments), you'll want to track every penny. Be sure to include any predictable income from side hustles, freelance work, or other sources, but be conservative—don't overestimate how much you'll earn from fluctuating or inconsistent streams.

If you're someone whose income varies from month to month, budgeting can be tricky. One option is to average your income over several months to get a realistic picture of what you typically bring in. Another strategy is to base your budget on your lowest-earning month, and treat any extra income as a bonus that you can save or use to pay off debt.

If you're expecting any windfalls—like a year-end bonus or tax refund—resist the urge to immediately factor it into your budget. Instead, treat these as unexpected extras, and allocate them to long-term savings or debt repayment when they actually hit your bank account—but not before.

### Build Your Budget Step 2:
### Track Your Expenses—Get Granular

Now that you've figured out your income, it's time to dive into your expenses. Here's where things get interesting. Some people like to budget using round numbers—"I spend about $500 on groceries each month"—while others prefer to get very granular.

Personally, I'm a fan of the granular approach, at least when I'm working with clients on a first-time budget. Why? Because getting down to the penny helps you understand exactly

MELISSA COX, CFP®

what's going out and gives you a clearer picture of where you might need to make changes.

When you get into the details of your expenses, you might be surprised by what you find. Let's take housing as an example. Sure, it's easy to lump your mortgage payment into one line in your budget, but are you really capturing the full cost of running your household?

I like to know everything about that mortgage. Are we escrowing for taxes and insurance? Are we paying PMI (Private Mortgage Insurance)? What's the cost of property taxes and homeowners insurance?

These details matter because you might be overlooking a big chunk of your expenses. By breaking them out, you can get a better understanding of where your money is going and find areas where you can make adjustments.

Another example is the way I like to budget for kids or other dependents. Separating expenses by child or family member you're caring for gives a much clearer picture. For instance, if you've got one child in daycare and another in school sports, those are very different costs, and they won't last forever. Eventually, those expenses will fall off your budget, freeing up room for other priorities. By getting specific, you can plan for how these changes will impact your financial future.

When it comes to budgeting, taxes are one area you can't afford to overlook. Not planning for taxes can put a major strain on your budget if you're hit with an unexpected bill come tax season. Setting aside funds throughout the year will keep your budget intact and prevent last-minute scrambles to cover your tax obligations.

If you own a business or have side gigs, budgeting for taxes is even more critical. Self-employed individuals are responsible for paying quarterly estimated taxes to avoid penalties and a hefty year-end bill. Factoring these payments into your regular expenses ensures you're prepared and won't be caught off guard.

Beyond setting aside funds, tax planning can also help you take advantage of deductions, credits, and tax-efficient strategies that could

## Private Mortgage Insurance (PMI)

Insurance that a mortgage lender might require you to buy if your down payment on a property is less than 20%—to protect the lender in case you default.

save you money. By incorporating tax planning into your budget, you'll have more control over your finances—and potentially keep more of what you earn.

So, how do you actually get the granular details of your expenses? Well, you've got options. One way is to comb through a year's worth of transactions from your bank and credit card statements. This method can be tedious, but it's a surefire way to capture every expense and see trends over time. You'll get a clear picture of those small, recurring charges that might be slipping through the cracks.

Another option is to download an app like Rocket Money, which can help you to automate the process. Rocket Money syncs with your bank accounts and automatically categorizes your spending. This is great for people who want to get detailed without manually tracking every purchase. You can even set up categories for things like mortgage, insurance, child expenses, and more.

MELISSA COX, CFP®

## Top-Down vs. Paycheck Cycle: What Works for You?

Some people prefer to approach budgeting from the top down—starting with their annual income and breaking it down into monthly and weekly expenses. This is a great method for those who feel comfortable looking at the big picture first and working backward. But let's face it: Many people don't actually know where their money goes, especially if they spend a lot of cash, which makes it hard to get a good idea of past expenses.

That's where paycheck cycle budgeting comes in. For those who struggle to track their spending, starting with your biggest monthly expenses (housing, transportation, insurance) and building a budget based on your paycheck schedule can be incredibly effective. You might even set a weekly budget to keep things manageable, or if necessary, a daily budget— which can feel a bit extreme but is helpful if you need strict discipline at the start.

Remember, budgeting is about practice, confidence, and self-control. If you need to start with a daily budget to get the hang of how you spend your money, that's perfectly fine! As you build better habits and become more comfortable, you'll find yourself graduating to weekly or even monthly budgets. Budgeting is a skill that gets better with time and experience.

One thing to watch out for while budgeting is the sneaky nature of credit cards. It's all too easy to let one stressful day or impulsive decision blow up an entire month's budget. But how do you know if you have a credit card problem?

Stop and compare your arm muscles. If your swiping arm looks like it's been hitting the gym while your non-swiping arm is still stuck on the couch, you might have a swiping habit.

Is it really tennis elbow, or are we talking about "swiping syndrome"? If your elbow aches after a day at the mall, it might be time to check if you're spending more time swiping than you think.

Do the employees at Costco know you on a first-name basis and get worried when they don't see you for a few days? If your local Costco staff starts asking if everything's okay when you haven't been in for a week, it's a good sign that credit cards might be ruling your life.

Seriously, for those who struggle with impulse spending, relying on credit cards can lead to dangerous debt traps. One stressful day or an unexpected "treat yourself" moment, and suddenly you've spent next month's grocery money on shoes you didn't need.

If this sounds familiar, you might want to try a cash-based budget or the envelope method—a system where you set aside a certain amount of cash for specific spending categories (like groceries or entertainment). Once it's gone for that month, it's gone. This can be a powerful way to strengthen your financial discipline and develop your money muscles—no extra swiping needed.

### Emergency Budgets: Planning for Curveballs

Let's be honest. Life is full of surprises. Some of them are good, like finding 20 bucks in an old coat pocket. But a lot of them are, well, less than ideal. Whether it's an unexpected medical bill, a car repair, or (heaven forbid) a global pandemic, having an emergency fund is what keeps you from having to rely on credit cards or loans when life throws a curveball.

Think of it as a financial fire drill. What can you live

MELISSA COX, CFP®

*Creating an emergency budget helps you identify the "wants" that have been quietly disguising themselves as "needs." Many people find a surprising sense of peace in discovering all the extras they really do not need.*

without if the income stops flowing? Do we really need four streaming services or that premium coffee subscription? Probably not. An emergency budget helps you identify the "wants" that have been quietly disguising themselves as "needs." And let me tell you, many people find a surprising sense of peace in figuring out that they don't need all the extras they thought they did.

So how much should you have in your emergency fund? An old rule of thumb is to aim for 3-to-6 months worth of living expenses. A more modern rule of thumb is to have approximately 12 months of living expenses available or flexible enough to access if needed. If that number sounds intimidating, don't worry. Start small, and build your way up. Even having $1,000 set aside can make a huge difference in an emergency. The important thing is to start saving. And once you've built up that cushion, you can rest a little easier.

As you build your emergency budget, think first about your needs:

- **Housing.** Your rent or mortgage is non-negotiable—you need a roof over your head.

- **Utilities**. Basic electricity, water, and heat are necessary, but maybe you can survive without all the bells and whistles of premium cable.
- **Groceries**. Food is a must, but perhaps now's the time to swap out the organic, artisanal snacks for more affordable staples.
- **Transportation**. If you rely on your car to get to work, that's a priority, but maybe cutting back on unnecessary trips can save gas money.

Then come the wants—those things that make life more comfortable but aren't critical to your survival. These might include:

- **Streaming services.** Do you really need Netflix, Hulu, Disney+, AppleTV *and* Amazon Prime? Probably not. Cutting back to one or two can make a difference.
- **Dining out or takeout.** Cooking at home is significantly cheaper than the GrubHub/DoorDash delivery fees, food, and tips. During tough times, this can be a big savings.
- **Subscription services**. From meal kits to premium music services, monthly subscriptions can add up. Canceling or pausing these can offer immediate relief.
- **Gym memberships or fitness classes**. There are plenty of free workout videos online that can replace expensive memberships,.

Once you've identified what can go, it's time to make a plan for how to cut back. Here's how you can go about trimming the fat in your budget when an emergency hits:

- **List Your Priorities.** Start by writing out your absolute essentials—the things you absolutely can't live without (housing, groceries, basic utilities, transportation). Then make a separate list of everything else that's non-essential, from streaming services to dining out.

- **Rank Your Discretionary Spending.** Not every "want" has to disappear immediately. Rank your discretionary spending by importance. Maybe keeping one streaming service is your compromise, but cutting the rest is manageable. Or perhaps dining out once a month is still within reason, but regular takeout has to go.

- **Cut or Pause Subscriptions.** One of the easiest ways to immediately cut costs is to cancel or pause monthly subscriptions. Whether it's your streaming services, gym membership, or meal delivery kit, these recurring expenses add up quickly. Most services allow you to pause without canceling, making it easier to jump back in once things stabilize.

- **Reevaluate Your Grocery Spending.** Groceries are necessary, but this is the time to get smart about it. Planning meals, buying in bulk, and switching to less expensive brands can free up extra money. Cutting out luxury items like prepackaged snacks or specialty ingredients can make a big impact over time.

- **Take a Look at Your Transportation Costs.** If you're commuting less due to a job loss or other life changes, now's the time to cut back on transportation costs. Carpooling, public transit, or biking can help save on gas. If you're really looking to slash expenses, consider parking your car and canceling non-essential insurance coverage temporarily (like collision on a non-driven vehicle). And if you live in a city with adequate public transportation, ask yourself whether or not you even need a car.

- **Communicate and Negotiate.** If the situation becomes more severe, don't hesitate to reach out and negotiate with service providers. Many companies are willing to offer temporary relief during hard times. This can include requesting a lower payment on utility bills, asking for a rent adjustment, or pausing services like Internet or cable without cancellation fees.

And hey, once you've gone through this process, don't be surprised if your emergency budget starts creeping into your current lifestyle. After all, cutting back on non-essentials and focusing on what truly matters can lead to a simpler, more mindful approach to spending. You might even find that living without all those extras isn't so bad—and that can free up even more money for the things that really matter, like reaching your financial goals faster.

### A Sample Budget from an Expert Financial Planner

Let's get real—budgeting can make or break your financial future. Whether you're fresh out of college, navigating your first job, or well into your career, having a budget is one of the most powerful tools you can use to ensure long-term financial success. One of the easiest times to learn how to budget is when you're transitioning from college to the so-called "real world." You've worked hard, you're getting job offers, and it's all incredibly empowering. But here's where temptation creeps in, and it can quickly lead you down a dangerous financial path.

A huge pet peeve of mine is seeing recent graduates locking themselves into massive expenses, like a shiny new sports car or a sprawling "McMansion," before they fully understand what they can realistically afford. It's so easy to think, "Hey, my income will grow over time, so I can afford to stretch a little now." But the truth is, you shouldn't bank on future income increases to cover current expenses. Learning smart money habits *before* making these major purchases is absolutely crucial. So, how do you figure out what's affordable? That's where a solid budget comes in.

Below is the sample budget I like to use for a person making $75,000 net a year. It's built around target percentages for major categories, ensuring that you're not overspending in one area at the expense of another. It's designed to help you balance your immediate needs with your long-term goals, so you can avoid the dreaded paycheck-to-paycheck cycle.

## Sample Budget

| Category | Target % | Annual | Monthly |
|---|---|---|---|
| Total Housing | 40.00% | $30,000.00 | $2,500.00 |
| Total Transportation | 10.00% | $7,500.00 | $625.00 |
| Total Household | 15.00% | $11,250.00 | $937.50 |
| Total Health | 5.00% | $3,750.00 | $312.50 |
| Total Savings | 10.00% | $7,500.00 | $625.00 |
| Total Debt Payments | 10.00% | $7,500.00 | $625.00 |
| Total Miscellaneous | 10.00% | $7,500.00 | $625.00 |
| Total | 100.00% | $75,000.00 | $6,250.00 |

## Expense Breakdown: What's in Each Category

To give you a better idea of where your money is going, here's a detailed breakdown of what I typically include under each category. This helps you cover all your bases and ensures no hidden expenses surprise you down the road.

## Total Housing (40%)

- Mortgage or Rent
- 2nd Mortgage or Line of Credit
- Property Taxes
- Homeowner's or Renter's Insurance
- Homeowner's Association Fees
- Home Warranty
- Home Repairs/Maintenance
- Utilities (Electricity, Water/Trash/Sewer, Gas/Propane)
- Cell Phones
- Pest Control, Landscaping, Pool Service
- Security/Alarm System

## Total Transportation (10%)

- Car Payment 1 and 2 (if applicable)
- Gas/Fuel
- Repairs/Maintenance
- Registration
- Car Insurance

## Total Household (15%)

- Groceries
- Toiletries/Household Supplies
- Childcare (if applicable)

## Total Health (5%)

- Medical, Dental, and Vision Insurance Premiums
- Medical Expenses and Copays

- Prescriptions
- Chiropractor Visits
- Massages (if medically necessary)

## Total Savings (10%)
- Emergency Fund
- 401(k) or IRA Contributions
- Stocks/Bonds/Mutual Funds
- College Fund Contributions
- Life Insurance
- Disability Insurance
- Miscellaneous Savings

## Total Debt Payments (10%)
- Credit Cards (1-5, if applicable)
- Student Loans (1-4, if applicable)
- Other Loans/Obligations

## Total Miscellaneous (10%)
- Entertainment (Movies, Streaming Services like Netflix, Hulu+)
- iTunes, eBooks, Apps, Games
- Cable/Landline/Internet
- Dry Cleaning, Housekeeping
- Gifts, Personal Grooming
- Gym Memberships
- Education/Training
- Dining Out, Lunches
- Charity Donations
- Clothing, Legal Fees, Tax Filing Fees
- Hobbies/Kids' Activities (Recurring and Irregular)

- Licensure/Endorsements, Subscriptions/Dues
- Vacations/Travel, Pet Care (Food, Supplies, Vet Bills, Grooming)

### *Training Takeaway: The Importance of Staying Flexible*

Budgeting isn't about depriving yourself; rather, it's about understanding your financial reality and making smart decisions. Sure, it's tempting to stretch your budget for a new car or for an apartment with all the bells and whistles, but that can backfire fast if you're not prepared.

As you progress in your career, your income will most likely grow, and that's great—but your budget needs to grow with you. Start by living within your means now, and over time, you'll build the financial foundation to afford the things you want without stressing about money.

# Understanding Your
# Financial Health

Let's start with something simple: your financial health. Now, I know that might sound a little like going to the doctor's office for a check-up (and who really enjoys that?). But trust me, this is much less painful. Just like you'd want to know how your body is doing, it's equally important to know how your money is doing.

But the good news? Once you have a clear picture of where you stand financially, you can start making decisions that will improve your situation, no matter where you're starting from.

Over the years, I've seen a lot of people who are hesitant to really dig into their finances. I get it—sometimes it feels like looking at your bank account or tallying up your debts is the last thing you want to do.

But just like with your health, pretending the problem isn't there doesn't actually solve anything. In fact, taking that first step to understand your financial health can be empowering. That's the moment you stop letting money control you and *you* start taking control of your money.

## Setting Realistic Financial Goals

Now that we're all feeling brave enough to look at our financial health—having organized our personal financial binder and made a budget—let's talk about setting goals. And here's the key word: *realistic*.

I've had clients come to me with goals that are all over the place—everything from "I want to retire at 40 and live on a yacht," to "I just want to get out of debt by the end of the year."

Look, I love ambition. But I'm also a big fan of being realistic. If you set goals that are too far out of reach, you'll only end up feeling discouraged. So let's start with something attainable.

Think about your financial priorities. Do you want to pay off debt? Save for a house? Build up an emergency fund? Whatever your goals are, make sure they're specific and measurable.

Instead of saying, "I want to save more," try something like, "I want to save $5,000 over the next year." That way, you have a clear target, and you can track your progress along the way. And believe me, there's nothing more satisfying than checking off a financial goal you've achieved.

### Evaluating Debt: A Plan for Tackling It

If there's one topic that tends to make people break out into a cold sweat, it's debt. Whether it's student loans, credit card balances, or that car loan that's hanging over your head, debt has a way of making you feel trapped. But here's the deal: Debt doesn't have to be forever. With the right plan, you can take control of it.

The first step is getting honest about how much debt you

MELISSA COX, CFP®

have. I know it's not a fun topic to think about, but you can't tackle a problem if you don't know exactly what the problem is. Write it all down—every balance, every interest rate. And then we'll start prioritizing.

There are a couple of different strategies for paying off debt, but two of the most common are the Debt Snowball and the Debt Avalanche methods. The Debt Snowball method focuses on paying off your smallest debts first so you get quick wins and build momentum. The Debt Avalanche method focuses on paying off the debt with the highest interest rate first, which saves you money on interest in the long run. Both methods work—it's just a matter of choosing the one that fits your personality and motivation.

Here's the key: Don't let debt paralyze you. I've had clients who were so overwhelmed by their debt that they didn't even want to open their credit card statements. But once they started attacking it—little by little—they realized that paying off debt is a marathon, not a sprint. And guess what? You absolutely can cross that finish line.

### Training Takeaway: Moving Forward with Confidence

By the end of this chapter, I hope you're feeling a little more confident and excited about beginning to understanding your financial health. It's not about being perfect—it's about knowing where you are, setting goals, and making a plan to get where you want to be. Whether you're just starting out or trying to get back on track, remember that every step you take brings you closer to financial freedom.

And if you're still feeling a little overwhelmed? That's okay. Financial planning is a journey, not a destination. You don't have to have it all figured out right now. But by taking the time to understand your financial health and creating a plan, you're already ahead of the game.

## Behavioral Finance—
## Mastering the Psychology of Money

When people think about financial planning, they often focus on the numbers—how much to save, where to invest, and how to grow wealth. And of course that makes sense. But there's another, often overlooked, factor that plays a huge role in your financial success: *your mindset*. It turns out that your emotions and psychological biases can have just as much of an impact on your financial decisions as your actual knowledge or skills.

This is the world of behavioral finance—a field that explores how psychology influences financial decisions.

Even the most rational person can fall into common traps like fear, overconfidence, or following the crowd. Understanding these psychological influences and learning how to manage them can help you make smarter, more rational choices with your money.

In this chapter, we'll dive into the most common behavioral biases that affect our financial decisions and discuss strategies to overcome them. The goal is to help you develop a mindset that fosters long-term success, even when your emotions try to lead you astray.

## The Emotional Side of Money

We like to think that we make decisions based purely on logic, but the truth is that money is deeply tied to our emotions. It's not just a tool for survival—money is tied to our sense of security, freedom, status, and even self-worth. As a result, it's easy to let feelings like fear, greed, and anxiety cloud our judgment. For example:

- **Fear** may cause you to sell your investments during a market downturn, locking in losses that might have been temporary.
- **Overconfidence** can lead you to take on too much risk, leading you to assume you can outsmart the market.
- **Stress** might drive you to avoid your finances altogether, sticking your head in the sand instead of confronting problems head-on.

These emotions are natural, but if left unchecked, they can undermine even the best-laid financial plans.

## Common Behavioral Biases in Finance

Let's break down some of the most common psychological biases that tend to influence our financial decisions—and learn how to avoid them.

- **Loss Aversion.** One of the most powerful biases is *loss aversion*, a tendency to feel the pain of a loss more intensely than the joy of a gain. Studies have shown that losing $100 feels much worse than gaining $100 feels good. This leads many people to make overly conservative financial decisions to avoid loss, even if taking a bit more risk could lead to higher rewards. To overcome it, recognize that market fluctuations and temporary losses are part of investing. Focus on your long-term goals instead of reacting to short-term losses. Remind yourself that taking calculated risks is a necessary part of growing wealth.

- **Confirmation Bias.** We all love to be right, and confirmation bias makes sure we only see evidence that supports our existing beliefs. This bias can lead you to focus on information that confirms your expectations while ignoring anything that contradicts them. For example, if you believe a particular investment is a winner, you might cherry-pick data that backs up your opinion while dismissing signs that it might not be so great after all. Challenge your assumptions. Seek out information and opinions that contradict your views. Surround yourself with diverse perspectives, and consult with experts who can provide objective insights. This practice will help you make more balanced, informed decisions.

- **Overconfidence.** Overconfidence bias can lead you to believe you have more control over the outcome of your investments than you actually do. You might think you can time the market, pick the next hot stock, or outsmart the pros. Unfortunately, this mindset can lead to taking on too much risk, making impulsive decisions, and ignoring warning signs. Acknowledge that no one can predict the market with certainty—not even the experts. Diversify your investments, and focus on long-term strategies rather than on trying to "beat the market." Trust in the power of consistency over time, rather than on risky, short-term gains.

- **Anchoring.** Anchoring happens when you rely too heavily on the first piece of information you receive, which can skew your decision-making. For example, if you hear that a stock is trading at $50 but used to be $100, you might think you're getting a bargain, even if $50 is still overvalued for the stock's true worth. Always evaluate investments based on their current value, not solely on past performance or on what you *hope* will happen. Keep your focus on objective data, like financial metrics and long-term trends, rather than getting stuck on initial impressions.

### Dealing with Financial FOMO (Fear of Missing Out)

We've all been there. You hear everyone talking about a hot new stock or a booming cryptocurrency, and suddenly, you feel like you're missing out on the opportunity of a lifetime. This is what's known as *Financial FOMO*—the "fear of missing out" on a potentially profitable investment. It can make you feel like you need to act fast or else you'll be left behind.

Financial FOMO is a common emotion, and it's a dangerous one. When you're driven by the fear of missing out, you're more likely to make impulsive decisions without doing the necessary research or considering how that investment fits into your overall financial plan. And often, by the time you hear about the "next big thing," it's already too late.

Financial FOMO taps into the *herd mentality* where you feel the urge to follow the crowd, believing that if everyone else is investing in something, it must be a good idea. The problem is that by the time you hear about a booming investment, much of the opportunity for profit may have already passed. The same goes for market bubbles—what goes up fast often comes down just as quickly.

How to combat financial FOMO? There are several ways:

- **Stick to Your Plan.** The best way to avoid getting swept up in the latest trend is to stick to your long-term financial plan. When you have clear goals and a strategy in place, you'll be less tempted to jump on every new investment that comes along.
- **Do Your Homework.** Before making any investment, make sure to research it thoroughly. Understand the risks, fees, and long-term potential, and ask yourself if it aligns with your goals. If the investment is truly a good opportunity, it will still be worth pursuing after you've taken the time to do your due diligence.
- **Diversify.** A diversified portfolio gives you exposure to different asset types and sectors which reduces the need to chase high-risk, high-reward investments. When your portfolio is balanced, you're less likely to feel like you're missing out because you already have a range of opportunities working for you.
- **Take a Breather:** If you feel that familiar rush of excitement or urgency, take a step back. Remind yourself that there will always be new investment opportunities, and that missing one won't make or break your financial future.

### The Dangers of Financial FOMO: A Cautionary Tale

I've seen firsthand how Financial FOMO can derail even the best-laid plans. One story from 2008 still weighs heavily on me.

During the financial crisis, I was working with a family whose broker had taken advantage of them; he was not looking out for their best interests. This broker had put them in risky investments without considering their actual needs or long-term goals. By the time they came to me, their portfolio was hemorrhaging and on life support.

The family was understandably distraught, and their 80-year-old patriarch, a retired professor, was feeling the financial pressure more than anyone. We worked hard to stop the losses, reallocating their remaining assets into a healthier, diversified portfolio that prioritized protection while still allowing for growth and appreciation. It wasn't a *quick* fix, but it was the *right* approach for their situation—safe, sustainable, and geared toward long-term recovery.

Unfortunately, Financial FOMO got the best of them.

Not long after we had stabilized their portfolio, the family was lured away by promises of immediate gains from another broker. They were told they could recoup their losses quickly if they just made one more aggressive move. Against my advice—against the advice of a fiduciary who is required to put the client's best interest first at all times—they decided to chase those high returns, convinced that it was the solution they had been looking for.

A year later, I found out they had lost everything. The professor, who should have been enjoying a peaceful retirement, was now working part-time at Walmart just to make ends meet. It was heartbreaking to see someone who had spent a lifetime in academia and in service to others now struggling financially, all because of the seductive pull of short-term promises.

The lesson here is clear: Chasing immediate gains can have devastating consequences, especially if it means stepping away from a well-thought-out plan. Financial FOMO can make people forget the value of steady, long-term growth and lead

MELISSA COX, CFP®

them into risks they can't afford to take. And unfortunately, those risks don't just cost money—they can steal the security and peace of mind that come from a sound financial strategy.

This story is a reminder that there's no shortcut to building lasting wealth. It's also a cautionary tale about the importance of working with a trustworthy financial advisor, ideally a fiduciary who is legally bound to act in your best interest.

In the financial world, not every broker has a fiduciary responsibility, which means some may prioritize commissions over what's best for you. In this case, the broker was not a fiduciary and profited whether or not the family's investments succeeded. It's a sad but powerful reminder that patience, discipline, and a solid, diversified plan are what keep your financial future intact.

Don't let the fear of missing out cause you to make decisions you'll regret. Stay focused on your goals. And I'll repeat: True financial success is a marathon, not a sprint.

### Strategies to Develop a Rational Financial Mindset

Now that you know some of the common psychological pitfalls, how do you develop a mindset that leads to smarter, more rational financial decisions? Here are some strategies to help you stay on track:

- **Create a Financial Plan and Stick to It.** Having a well-thought-out financial plan is your best defense against emotional decisions. When markets fluctuate or you're tempted to jump on a trendy investment, refer back to your plan and remember why you made your original choices. A solid plan helps you stay grounded during volatile times.
- **Take a Long-Term View.** One of the most effective ways

to avoid emotional investing is to focus on the long-term. Short-term market swings are normal, and reacting to them can hurt your portfolio more than help. By keeping your eyes on the horizon, you're less likely to make panic-driven decisions.

- **Automate Where You Can.** Automation can be your best friend when it comes to avoiding emotional investing. Set up automatic contributions to your savings and retirement accounts so that you don't have to make decisions in the heat of the moment. This way, you can continue building your wealth without the temptation to stop or adjust based on short-term emotions.

- **Check in With a Financial Advisor.** Sometimes we're too close to our own finances to see things clearly. A trusted financial advisor—a fiduciary—can provide the objective, rational perspective you need to stay on course. They can also help you assess risks, adjust your strategy when needed, and remind you of your long-term goals when emotions start to take over.

> *Chasing immediate gains can have devastating consequences, especially if it means stepping away from a well-thought-out plan.*

- **Practice Financial Mindfulness.** Mindfulness isn't just for yoga; it's a valuable tool in financial planning, too. When you feel emotions like fear or excitement driving your financial decisions, take a step back. Ask yourself if

MELISSA COX, CFP®

your choices are based on data and long-term goals or if they're being driven by short-term feelings or that one article you just read by an author without a financial background. By practicing mindfulness, you can create space to make more thoughtful decisions.

### Training Takeaway: Own Your Financial Mindset

The good news is that you don't have to be an emotional victim when it comes to money. By recognizing the biases and psychological traps that affect your financial decisions, you can take back control and make smarter, more rational choices.

Remember, building wealth is as much about mindset as it is about money management. By keeping a clear head, challenging your assumptions, and sticking to a long-term plan, you'll be able to navigate the ups and downs of the financial world with confidence.

So the next time the markets get a little shaky or you feel the pull of the latest investment trend, take a deep breath, revisit your plan with a fiduciary advisor, and trust in the steady path you've created for yourself.

## Overcoming Financial Myths
## and Mental Barriers

Alright, let's talk about the elephants in the room. You know the ones—they're the financial myths, misconceptions, and mental roadblocks that keep popping up, making you feel like financial planning is way harder than it needs to be. Over the years I've heard it all. Clients tell me things like, "I can't afford a financial planner," or "I'm just not good with money," or my personal favorite, "I'll just deal with my finances later."

These are the kinds of beliefs that can keep you from achieving financial success—not because they're true, but because they *feel* true. And once they take root in your mind, they can really hold you back. So in this chapter, we're going to break down some of the most common financial myths and tackle the mental barriers that tend to get in the way. Don't worry, I'll help you clear these roadblocks so you can move forward with confidence.

### Myth #1: "Financial Planning is Expensive"

I get it—when you hear "financial planner," you might picture someone in a high-rise office, wearing a fancy suit, charging you thousands of dollars just to talk about retirement. But here's the truth: Financial planning isn't just for the wealthy, and it's definitely not out of reach for most people. Working with a financial planner can actually save you money in the long run.

Without a clear strategy, it's easy to overspend, miss out on tax-saving opportunities, or invest without understanding the risks. A good financial planner helps you avoid these common pitfalls by creating a plan tailored to your needs. They can help you budget smarter, reduce costs, and optimize your investments—all which add up over time. Whether you're managing debt, saving for a house, or planning for retirement, professional guidance can make a big difference.

And here's a secret: There are a lot of ways to get financial advice that won't break the bank. Some planners offer flat fees, others work on a percentage of your assets, and some even offer hourly rates. There are also plenty of resources, like online financial planning tools, that can help you get started without spending a fortune.

Financial planning is more accessible than ever, so don't let the cost hold you back from securing your financial future.

### Myth #2: "I'm Not Good With Money"

I hear this one a lot, and every time I do, I want to sit that person down and say, "Let's break this down." The truth is, no one is *born* knowing how to manage money. It's a skill, just like learning to cook or drive (and I bet some of us remember those early driving lessons—yikes!). The good news? You don't have to be a financial wizard to manage your money well.

It just takes a few lessons, some practice, and a whole lot of patience.

Most people think they're "bad with money" because they've made a few mistakes or they don't understand all the jargon that gets thrown around in the financial world. But guess what? Making mistakes is part of the process. I've been a financial planner for decades, and I still learn something new just about every day. The key is being willing to learn and not letting those early missteps scare you off.

> Time is one of the most powerful tools in financial planning. The longer you wait to start saving, investing, or paying off debt, the harder it becomes to catch up.

If you're feeling overwhelmed by your finances, start small. You don't need to tackle everything at once. Break it down into manageable steps—like creating a simple budget, paying off one credit card, or setting up an automatic transfer to your savings account. Every little bit helps, and before you know it, you'll feel a lot more confident about managing your money.

### Myth #3: "I'll Deal With My Finances Later"

Ah, procrastination's favorite excuse: "I'll get to it later." Sound familiar? Here's the thing: Waiting to deal with your finances is a lot like ignoring that weird noise your car is making. Sure, you can put it off for a while, but eventually, it's going to get louder and more expensive to fix.

MELISSA COX, CFP®

The earlier you start taking control of your finances, the easier it is to get where you want to go. That's because time is one of the most powerful tools in financial planning. The longer you wait to start saving, investing, or paying off debt, the harder it becomes to catch up. But the sooner you start—even if it's just with small steps—the more time you give yourself to build wealth, take advantage of compound growth, and reach your goals.

If you've been putting off dealing with your finances because you're too busy or you feel like you don't have enough money to get started, let me tell you something. There's no such thing as the perfect time. Life is always busy, and you don't need a big lump sum to start planning for your future. You just need to start.

### And Then There Are Your Feelings

As we said previously, money is deeply tied to our emotions, and for many people, that's where the real challenge lies. I've had clients who were excellent at math and knew all the right things to do, but they still struggled because of their emotional relationship with money.

Maybe you've heard the term "money dysmorphia"— that's when your perception of your financial situation doesn't match reality. For example, you might be doing well financially, but you still feel like you're always broke. Or maybe the opposite is true—you've been avoiding your bank account and think everything's fine, but your debt is quietly piling up in the background.

Social media plays a huge role in this mindset. We're constantly bombarded with images of people who seem to be living their best lives—new cars, exotic vacations, fancy dinners. It can make you feel like you're falling behind, even if you're doing just fine. This comparison trap can lead to overspending, financial stress, and a never-ending cycle of feeling like you're not "enough."

Here's my advice: Take a step back. Your financial journey is your own (*your race, your pace*, remember?). Don't compare your situation to anyone else's. Everyone has different priorities, goals, and circumstances, and the only thing that really matters is that you're making progress toward *your* goals.

### Strategies to Shift Your Mindset

If you've been struggling with the emotional side of money, here are a few strategies to help you shift your mindset:

- **Practice financial gratitude.** Take a moment to appreciate what you have, rather than focusing on what you don't have. Maybe you're not where you want to be yet, but you're taking steps in the right direction—and that's worth celebrating.
- **Set boundaries with social media**. It's easy to fall into the comparison trap when you're constantly scrolling through other people's highlight reels. Limit your exposure, and remind yourself that what you see online isn't always an accurate reflection of reality.
- **Track your progress**. One of the best ways to shift your mindset is to track your financial wins—no matter how small. Paid off a credit card? Celebrate. Hit a savings goal? Give yourself a pat on the back. These small victories will build your confidence and help you see how far you've come.

MELISSA COX, CFP®

*Training Takeaway:*
*Clearing Roadblocks and Building Confidence*

It's easy to get caught up in financial myths and emotional barriers, but the good news is that once you recognize them, you can overcome them. Financial planning doesn't have to be expensive, complicated, or stressful. And you don't have to be "good with money" to be successful with your finances. You just need to take it one step at a time.

By now, you've got some tools to start clearing away those mental roadblocks and moving toward your financial goals with confidence. Remember, financial success isn't about being perfect—it's about making consistent progress and staying committed to your plan.

So let's leave those myths behind and keep moving forward. You've got this.

## The Cost of Convenience:
### How "Easy Living" is Draining Our Wallets

Let's face it—life is easier now than ever before. Groceries? Delivered. Dinner? Delivered. Your favorite shoes in two different colors because you can't decide which looks better? Delivered. Convenience is the name of the game, and we've been playing it for decades. But here's the truth: While this instant gratification feels great in the moment, it comes with a hefty price tag—one that's slowly but surely draining our wallets.

It's not just a 21st-century problem, either. Every generation has grappled with the allure of convenience in one form or another. We've gone from brick-and-mortar stores to the explosion of fast food, and now, to the era of one-click shopping and on-demand delivery. But while the method may have evolved, the mindset remains the same—if it's easy and fast, we want it. And if we want it, we're willing to pay for it.

### Convenience Has a Price—
### And It's Sneakier Than You Think

When was the last time you stopped to think about what all this convenience is costing you? Sure, it's just a few dollars

MELISSA COX, CFP®

extra to have your groceries delivered, and what's a couple of dollars for a delivery fee on your late-night pizza? But when you start adding it all up—delivery fees, surge pricing, subscription costs—those "convenience charges" begin to pile up in ways we rarely anticipate.

Let's say you're ordering food a couple of times a week through a delivery app like FAVOR. You're paying for the meal, tipping the driver, and covering the delivery fee. If you're like most people, you justify it by thinking, "It's saving me time!" But multiply that by 52 weeks a year, and suddenly, you're spending hundreds—if not thousands—on something you could have picked up yourself. And that's just one small area of spending.

In a world where we can have nearly anything we want with minimal effort, convenience becomes addictive. We start to *believe* that time is money and that spending a little extra here and there is justified if it saves us time.

But let's be honest, convenience isn't just about time—it's about instant gratification. The thrill of getting what we want when we want it is deeply satisfying. From streaming services to rideshares, we've become conditioned to expect things immediately. Waiting feels like a waste of time, and in a fast-paced world, anything that slows us down feels like an inconvenience.

### A Real-Life Example: "Eating at Home" Isn't Always What It Seems

Let me share a story about a young couple I once worked with who came to me because they wanted help learning to budget. In our initial conversation, they confidently told me that they ate most of their meals at home and didn't believe in using delivery services. They sounded like a budgeting dream—cooking meals at home *and* avoiding the high costs of dining out or delivery fees.

So, imagine my surprise when I took a closer look at their spending and found that their food budget was a whopping $3,000 a month for just the two of them. Yes, you read that correctly—three grand every month, just on food!

Even more shocking? When I asked them about it, they explained that they were "technically" eating at home. How? Well, they would stop by restaurants on their way home from work, pick up their favorite takeout, and bring it home to eat at their kitchen table. To them, this was "eating at home"— just with food someone else had cooked.

The irony wasn't lost on me. Here they were, thinking they were saving money by skipping delivery and sitting down at home to eat. But in reality, they were paying restaurant prices for nearly every meal. It was a classic case of convenience spending sneaking into their budget, disguised as something more reasonable.

### From Fast Food to Fast Everything: How Convenience Has Evolved

Let's rewind to the early days of convenience. Back when fast food was the big revolution, families were excited about the idea of getting a less expensive meal for the whole family without stepping foot in a restaurant. You could say this was the gateway drug to convenience spending—it was quick, it was easy, and it felt justified because "everyone's doing it."

Fast forward to today, and fast food is just the tip of the

> There's convenience at every turn now, and it's no longer just about food—it's about every aspect of our lives. But the cost? Well, that's gone up significantly, too.

iceberg. Now, we have everything from same-day shipping, to meal delivery kits that eliminate the need to even think about what to cook. There's convenience at every turn, and it's no longer just about food—it's about every aspect of our lives.

As a financial planner, I've seen this evolution firsthand. I went from trying to help families cut back on eating out, to now helping them avoid using delivery apps for every meal or item. And trust me, it's not easy convincing someone to skip the "easy button" when it's so deeply embedded into their daily habits.

### Convenience vs. Budget:
### When Easy Living Hurts Your Long-Term Goals

Here's the harsh reality: When your budget is stretched thin, convenience spending becomes a real problem.

It's not usually the big-ticket items that blow up your finances—it's the constant little charges—the $5 delivery fee here, the $20 convenience upgrade there—that add up over time. Keeping convenience spending in check doesn't mean cutting out every treat, but it does mean being mindful of how these frequent and "harmless" expenses are silently stacking up against your long-term financial success.

Let's say you're saving for a vacation or trying to build an emergency fund. Cutting back on unnecessary convenience spending can be a game-changer. It's not about eliminating convenience from your life altogether; rather, it's about being intentional with when and how you indulge in it.

Start by asking yourself a simple question: "Is this convenience worth the cost?" There are times when paying for convenience makes sense, like when you're in a pinch or when your time is worth more than the money you're spending. But when convenience becomes a long-term habit, that's when it's time to reassess.

### Training Takeaway: Prioritize Purpose Over Convenience

This may sound *conveniently* familiar, but in a world where convenience is everywhere, those easy choices can quietly derail your financial goals. By making more thoughtful choices, you can save money without sacrificing too much of that precious time you're always chasing.

At the end of the day, convenience is like dessert—great in moderation but bad for your health (and budget) if you indulge too often. So the next time you reach for your phone to order dinner or opt for that express shipping, remember: It's your race, your pace. And sometimes, the slower route might be the one that gets you to your goals faster.

# Planning

## The Importance of a Financial Plan and the Appropriate Advisor

Let me start by saying this again because it's worth repeating: If you don't have a financial plan yet, you're not alone. In fact, most people I meet didn't start with a plan. For a lot of folks, financial planning feels like something they'll get to "eventually"—right after they figure out what exactly their 401(k) is, or when they have "enough" money to start investing.

But here's the truth: Waiting for the perfect moment to plan your finances is like waiting for the perfect time to start going to the gym.

Spoiler alert—there's never a perfect time. You just have to dive in.

So let's talk about why having a financial plan is so important, no matter where you are in life. A plan isn't a rigid, overwhelming document that locks you into a lifetime of boring money choices.

Instead, think of it as your road map—it guides you toward the future you want while still allowing room for life to happen, because trust me, life always happens.

MELISSA COX, CFP®

## Why Comprehensive Financial Planning
## Is More Than Just Investments

When people hear "financial planning," they often think it's just about picking the right investments and watching the numbers grow. Don't get me wrong; investments are a big part of it. But a good financial plan is so much more than that. It's about taking a big-picture look at every aspect of your financial life: your income, your savings, your debt, your insurance, your future goals. It's like building a puzzle. Investments are just one piece, and you need all the other pieces to make the whole thing work.

A financial plan covers everything from saving for a rainy day (or maybe a not-so-rainy one, like your future dream home) to making sure you're protected if something unexpected happens. It looks at how your finances today are going to shape your tomorrow, whether that's five years or twenty-five years down the road.

When you build a comprehensive plan, you're es-

> Without a plan, it's easy to fall into the trap of impulsive financial decisions, especially when life throws you curveballs. You can end up reacting to short-term problems instead of planning for long-term success.

sentially giving yourself options. Want to take a sabbatical in a few years to travel? A plan can help you budget for that. Want to start your own business down the line? A plan can help you figure out how much you'll need. Planning is about creating flexibility so that you can live the life you want without constantly worrying about money.

## Common Mistakes People Make Without a Plan

I can't tell you how many clients have come to me over the years feeling totally stressed out about their finances, not because they weren't earning enough, but because they didn't have a plan. Without a plan, people tend to make the same mistakes repeatedly. They might spend more than they earn, let debts pile up, or invest in things that don't align with their long-term goals.

One of the biggest mistakes I see is people treating financial decisions as separate, disconnected events. They might decide to buy a new car or take a vacation without considering how those choices fit into the bigger picture of their financial health. It's like trying to bake a cake without following the recipe—you might end up with something tasty, but it's not going to be the masterpiece you were hoping for.

Without a plan, it's easy to fall into the trap of impulsive financial decisions, especially when life throws you curveballs. You can end up reacting to short-term problems instead of planning for long-term success. And here's the thing: Without a clear plan, it's also really hard to know if you're making progress toward your goals. You could be doing all the "right" things—saving, investing, budgeting—but if it's not part of a larger strategy, you might not get the results you want.

MELISSA COX, CFP®

## Building a Plan That Evolves With You

Let me be super clear: A financial plan is not a one-and-done deal. It's not something you set up and forget about. In fact, the best financial plans are the ones that evolve with you. Just like your life changes, your financial plan should change, too.

Maybe you started your plan when you were single and focused on paying off student loans, but now you're married and thinking about buying a house. Or maybe you've hit that magical point in life where you no longer need to budget for diapers and daycare (hallelujah!). Whatever the case, your financial needs will shift over time, and your plan should shift with them.

That's why I like to think of financial planning as a living document. It's something you revisit regularly—adjusting as needed when your goals or circumstances change. And hey, life is unpredictable, so don't worry if you need to course-correct along the way. The important thing is that you have a structure in place that can adapt as you do.

## Finding the Appropriate Guide for Your Financial Plan

Okay, so now you know *why* a financial plan is important. Let's talk about *how* to actually create one. I'm not going to lie and say it's going to be the most thrilling Saturday afternoon of your life, but the payoff (pun intended) is worth it.

First of all, please remember that you don't have to do this planning alone. A financial planner can help guide you through the process making sure your plan is tailored to your specific needs and goals. Only a Certified Financial Planner™ (CFP®) has met the rigorous qualifications and has the experience, and fiduciary responsibility to truly put your best interests first. Finding a CFP® is the best way to ensure you're getting advice from someone who knows their stuff *and* is legally committed to putting you first.

Of course, not every CFP® professional operates the same way in every scenario, which is why I encourage you to ask the thoughtful questions

> A financial plan is not a one-and-done deal. It's not something you set up and forget about. In fact, the best financial plans are the ones that evolve with you. Just like your life changes, your financial plan should change, too.

in this chapter to find someone who truly aligns with your goals and values. Transparency is key, and your trust should never be taken for granted.

Not all advice is created equal. Understanding whether you need an investment-focused professional or a comprehensive financial planner is critical:

- **Financial Advice.** This involves creating a comprehensive plan or making specific recommendations based on your unique situation. A fiduciary professional giving financial advice *must* put your best interests first.
- **Non-Financial Advice Related to Money**. Non-financial advice is more transactional and often involves helping you purchase products or services, like life insurance, without a

broader financial plan. In this case, the fiduciary standard might not apply, and the suitability standard—ensuring the product fits your needs—may be the only requirement.

- **Investment Advice**. An investment advisor typically focuses on managing your investments rather than broader financial planning. Investment advisors registered with the SEC or state regulators are legally required to act as fiduciaries when providing investment advice. However, the scope of their services might not include areas like tax planning or estate strategies.

Now that you know the types of advice you might encounter, it's time to meet the players. These organizations exist to help you find professionals who are trained, trustworthy, and ready to guide you:

- **CFP Board (Certified Financial Planner Board of Standards)**. The CFP Board regulates and certifies professionals who have earned the CFP® designation. You can use their searchable directory at cfp.net to find Certified Financial Planners in your area. CFP® professionals are trained to provide comprehensive financial planning, must act as fiduciaries when offering financial advice, and must complete continuing education to maintain certification. However, they may operate under different compensation models, so it's important to clarify their approach upfront.
- **NAPFA (National Association of Personal Financial Advisors)**. If you're looking for a financial advisor who's allergic to commissions, NAPFA is your spot. Their Find-an-Advisor tool at napfa.org ensures you'll find advisors who are strictly fee-only and act as fiduciaries. They're all about transparency and putting clients first.
- **NACFF (National Association of Certified Financial Fiduciaries)**. For those seeking a fiduciary-focused

professional—whether fee-only, commission-based, or hybrid—NACFF might be your go-to. Their directory, available at nationalcffassociation.org, connects you with professionals who have earned the Certified Financial Fiduciary® (CFF) designation. They're trained to prioritize your interests first, no matter their compensation model.

### Questions to Ask When Choosing an Advisor

Once you've identified potential planners or advisors, asking the right questions can help you find someone who fits your needs. Use this list as a guide:

- **Are you a fiduciary?** This ensures the planner is legally obligated to act in your best interest.
- **What are your qualifications and areas of expertise?** Look for certifications such as CFP®, CFF®, or NAPFA membership, and ask about their experience with clients in similar situations.
- **How are you compensated?** Planners may be fee-only, commission-based, or a combination of both. Fee-only planners avoid conflicts of interest by receiving payment directly from clients rather than earning commissions.
- **What is your investment philosophy?** Their approach should align with your goals, risk tolerance, and time horizon. For example, do they prefer active or passive management strategies?
- **Do you offer discretionary management, or do I retain control of my accounts?** Some planners have discretionary authority, allowing them to make trades or adjustments without your prior approval. Others consult you

MELISSA COX, CFP®

before making changes. Choose the level of involvement you're comfortable with.

- **How do you align financial plans with personal values or beliefs?** If ethical investing, ESG strategies, or cultural principles are important to you, ask how they incorporate those into their planning process.
- **What types of clients do you typically work with?** Ensure the planner has experience working with individuals in similar financial situations or life stages, such as retirees, small business owners, or young professionals.
- **How will we communicate, and how often?** It's important to know how accessible they'll be and whether updates will come through regular meetings, phone calls, or emails.
- **What services do you provide beyond investment management?** Comprehensive planners often offer additional services like tax planning, retirement strategies, estate planning, and more.
- **What's your personal philosophy on wealth and financial planning?** This question provides insight into their values and approach, helping you determine whether their mindset aligns with your own goals and beliefs.
- **Can you explain your client onboarding process?** A clear and organized onboarding process can indicate professionalism and a client-centered approach.
- **What happens if I decide to end our relationship?** Understanding their process for transferring accounts or disengaging can save potential headaches in the future.

You do not have to work with a certified financial professional. But for the love of all things holy, please work with *someone* qualified—not someone's cousin who's watched a few YouTube videos and now thinks he's Warren Buffett.

## How to Create Your Own Financial Plan

Whether or not you'll be working with a CFP®, here are some steps to get you started on your personal financial plan:

- **Take stock of where you are now.** Look at your current financial health—your income, savings, debts, and any assets you own. Think of this step as your starting point on the map.
- **Set your financial goals.** What do you want to achieve? Be specific. Maybe it's paying off your student loans in five years or saving for a down payment on a house. Your goals will guide the direction of your plan.
- **Create a budget that works.** This step is your financial GPS. A budget will show you how much you can allocate towards your goals each month. Don't worry, you can still have room for fun—it's all about balance!
- **Plan for the unexpected.** Build an emergency fund if you haven't already. Trust me, your future self will thank you.
- **Invest with purpose.** Think about how your investments align with your goals. If you're planning for retirement, make sure your portfolio reflects that long-term goal. If you're planning for something sooner, like buying a house, your investment strategy might look different.
- **Review and adjust.** This is where you check in with your plan every few months or after a big life event. Did you get a raise? Adjust your budget. Did you welcome a new family member? Time to revisit those long-term goals.

## Can AI Replace Human Financial Planners?

With the rapid rise of technology, you've probably heard that Artificial Intelligence (AI) is creeping into nearly every industry, including financial services. Robo-advisors and AI-powered platforms have made it easier to automate investments and financial decisions, leading some to wonder: Will AI replace human financial planners?

The short answer: probably not.

While AI is fantastic for data-driven tasks and crunching numbers, there's one element it can't replace—human connection. Financial planning is about more than just numbers; it's deeply personal, emotional, and unique to each individual.

Money is an emotional topic for most people. Whether it's dealing with financial stress, navigating life transitions like retirement, or handling the pressure of debt, emotions are often a driving force behind financial decisions. My best meetings with clients have had us both laughing and crying—because that's what real financial conversations are like. They're personal, they're raw, and they go beyond what a robo-advisor could ever provide. Plus, water and electronics don't mix well, and a fiery explosion or short circuit might not be the best way to end a meeting—although it would be quite the commotion in testing everyone's ability to rapidly respond! AI simply can't replicate the level of empathy and human understanding that people are looking for.

AI can analyze your spending patterns and suggest investments, but it can't fully understand your goals, dreams, or unique situation. Human planners tailor their advice to your individual needs, family dynamics, and life stages. They can ask the right questions and offer nuanced advice that a robo-advisor can't.

Major life events—like marriage, having children, buying a home, or starting a business—are complicated, and the financial implications vary greatly from person to person. Human financial planners excel at helping clients navigate these complexities, providing guidance that takes into account both the financial and emotional aspects of big life decisions.

> ## Artificial Intelligence (AI)
>
> A technology that allows computers and machines to simulate human intelligence and problem-solving capabilities.

As we've said before, financial planning isn't a one-time event; it's an ongoing relationship that evolves with you. Human planners can anticipate your needs as your life changes, adjusting your plan to reflect those changes in real-time. That level of long-term commitment and foresight is something AI just doesn't offer.

While AI and robo-advisors have their place, especially when it comes to simplifying investments and offering convenience, they can't replace the personal, empathetic, and flexible approach that human financial planners bring to the table.

Yes, I use tools and algorithms to help quantify goals, assess risk, and sort through investment options because there's no way to handle the sheer volume of data without them. Algorithms may crunch the numbers, but they don't understand the significance of helping you plan for your family's future or know when to share a laugh (or a tear) with you during a meaningful financial conversation. In a world full of complex tech, you still need a real person to guide you through life's financial ups and downs.

MELISSA COX, CFP®

*Training Takeaway:*
*Building Confidence for a Secure Financial Future*

By now, I hope you're feeling excited (okay, maybe a little less nervous) about finding the right advisor and starting to build your financial plan. It doesn't have to be complicated or intimidating. In fact, once you start, you'll probably wonder why you didn't do it sooner. A solid financial plan provides clarity and peace of mind giving you the confidence to enjoy today, knowing you're also investing in tomorrow.

So grab your financial toolkit, put on your metaphorical hard hat, and let's start building that plan. After all, *it's your race, at your pace*—and this is one race where the prize is a financially secure future.

## Goal Planning: Dream Big, Plan Smart

I know, it sounds obvious—of course, everyone has financial goals, right? But when we dig a little deeper, many people realize they haven't really mapped out what those goals are, let alone thought about how to achieve them.

So let's talk about it, because the truth is, goal setting isn't just about ticking boxes. It's about dreaming a little, thinking outside the box, and crafting a road map to help you not only reach financial stability but also live the life you've always wanted.

### The SMART Approach to Goal Planning

Let's start with a tried-and-true strategy for setting goals: SMART goals. SMART stands for Specific, Measurable, Achievable, Relevant, and Time-bound. It's a simple framework that ensures your goals aren't just vague ideas floating in your mind, but actionable steps that lead to real progress.

- **Specific**: Your goals need to be crystal clear. For example, instead of saying, "I want to save money," say, "I want to save $10,000 for a down payment on a home."

- **Measurable**: How will you track progress? Make sure your goal has metrics attached to it, like saving $500 a month toward that $10,000.
- **Achievable**: Your goals should be challenging but realistic. No sense setting yourself up for failure. If saving $500 a month is a stretch, adjust it to something more manageable.
- **Relevant**: Does this goal align with your life and values? If homeownership is important, then saving for a down payment is relevant. If travel is your passion, maybe the goal is about funding an adventure.
- **Time-bound**: Set a timeline. Saying "I want to save $10,000 by the end of the year" gives you a clear deadline to work toward.

SMART goals help you break big dreams into manageable steps. They provide direction and purpose, ensuring you're not just drifting along but actively working toward something meaningful.

### The Three Tiers of Planning

It's important to break down your goals into three categories: short-term, mid-term, and long-term. Each serves a different purpose, and together they create a balanced plan that keeps you moving forward, both in the immediate and distant future.

- **Short-term goals** can typically be accomplished within the next year or two. These goals might include paying off a credit card, building an emergency fund, or saving for a vacation. These goals are more immediate, and reaching them helps build momentum.

- **Mid-term goals** are set for the next 3-7 years. These could involve buying a house, saving for a child's education, or starting your own business. They're big enough to require planning but close enough that you can see them on the horizon.
- **Long-term goals** are those you plan for 7+ years into the future. This is where retirement often fits in, but it could also include larger dreams like building a dream home or setting up a legacy for your family. These goals require discipline, vision, and patience.

Each of these goal categories plays a vital role in your financial journey. You can't just focus on the long-term and ignore the here and now, nor can you get stuck only thinking about what's right in front of you. A well-rounded plan keeps you focused across all timelines, making sure today's efforts pay off tomorrow.

### Dream a Little: Goals Aren't Just About Retirement

Here's where I like to have a little fun. Most people think of financial goals as something serious, like saving for retirement or paying down debt, and while those are important, they're not the whole picture. Goals should also be about passion, adventure, and living life to the fullest. After all, this is your life—*your race, your pace.*

I always encourage clients to dream a little when it comes to goal setting. What do you really want out of life? Is there a passion project you've always wanted to pursue? A place you've dreamed of visiting? A hobby you've wanted to turn into

MELISSA COX, CFP®

something more? These are just as important as the financial goals you set for retirement or a rainy-day fund.

Goals don't always have to be about practicalities like saving for a house or retirement. They can also be about finding the freedom to do something you've always dreamed of, like quitting your job to start a business or spending a year traveling the world. By getting clients to think outside the box, I see them come alive with a new purpose—not just head down, working toward retirement, but excited about what's possible in the here and now.

### Training Takeaway: Goals Are Your Road Map to Living Life on Your Terms

When we set goals, we're giving ourselves permission to dream big while creating a road map to make those dreams a reality. Whether you're aiming for short-term wins, mid-term milestones, or long-term legacy planning, having clear goals in place is the best way to stay on track.

But remember, it's not just about achieving financial security. It's about living life to the fullest and finding joy along the way. So set those SMART goals, dream a little bigger, and let's work toward something that excites you—whether that's a passion project, a new adventure, or even just more time to do what you love. After all, as you now have read it several times, *it's your race, your pace.*

# Tiny Humans, Big Expenses: The Financial Realities of Raising Kids

You might have thought I would lump kids into the budgeting chapter, right? Well, not so fast. Kids are such a unique and monumental part of life that they deserve their own chapter. When it comes to finances, children take the spotlight in ways that go far beyond line items in a budget—they require planning, strategy, and maybe even a little magic... okay, a *lot* of magic. From the moment you start thinking about having children, the financial planning begins. And spoiler alert: It doesn't stop until well into their adulthood.

One of the most common discussions I have with clients is about planning for children. Some people come in wanting to plan everything out to the final dollar, determined to budget every aspect of parenthood way before they even have children. Others take a different approach—they want to delay having kids until they feel "ready," financially or otherwise.

The truth is, you're never fully ready for kids, no matter how well you plan. Kids are the ultimate wild card, and while financial planning can certainly help, there's no way to prepare for everything they'll bring into your life—both the joy and the chaos.

## The Cost of Raising a Child: Let's Talk Numbers

Let's get straight to the numbers: According to the United States Department of Agriculture, the average cost of raising a child from birth to age 18 in 2024 is approximately $233,000. That's right, about a quarter of a million dollars!! And just to be clear, this doesn't even include college expenses, which can add tens of thousands more to the overall cost.

Some of the biggest costs hit early, especially when it comes to childcare. For instance, full-time infant care in 2025 is expected to cost around $1,900 per month—but it can vary widely depending on where you live. That's nearly $23,000 per year just for someone to care for your baby while you work! And then there are other everyday expenses that come into play from day one.

Let's break it down according to 2024 prices:

- **Diapers**. You'll likely spend around $900 to $1,000 a year per child on diapers alone, which comes out to about $80 per month. That's roughly 3,000 diapers a year for each child.

- **Formula**. If you're not breastfeeding, baby formula can cost you between $1,200 to $3,600 annually. And before you think breastfeeding might save you money, there are still costs to consider. Between pumps, storage bags, bottles, nursing bras, and endless snacks for mom, the expenses add up—not including the cost of time! Speaking from experience. breastfeeding is a full-time job in itself. It turns out feeding a baby is expensive no matter how you do it!

- **Socks**. But perhaps the most puzzling (and expensive) item you'll buy for your child? Socks. Yes, those tiny, adorable socks that disappear faster than you can say, "Where's the other one?" You'll buy pack after pack, only for them to vanish into thin air. Maybe that's where the real money goes.

## The "Baby Stuff" Trap: Keep a Cool Head

Now, let's talk about the baby market, which is massive. Walk into any baby store, and you'll be surrounded by gadgets, gizmos, and gear—everything from high-tech bassinets that can rock your baby to sleep, to designer cribs that could almost rival a luxury car in price. And let's face it, everything is adorable, making it hard to resist.

But adorable doesn't always mean practical. I urge you to keep a cooler head and stay practical when stocking your house with baby gear. Sure, that top-of-the-line crib might look fabulous in your nursery, but it won't help your baby sleep any better than a more affordable one that's just as safe. Let's also give a shout-out to the designer outfit that kids wear once or twice for a few hours before outgrowing it.

Pro-Parenting tip: I absolutely allowed my younger daughter to wear her fancy "princess" party dress to preschool because I did not want it to go to waste. It made her feel like she was living her best 3-year-old life. Mom win!

And those $100+ satin fitted sheets? They'll feel utterly ridiculous the first time your baby has a blowout in the middle of the night, ruining the sheets and everything else in its path (and yes, that stuff is hard to get out...literally).

The point is, don't let pregnancy purchases derail your baby budget. Stick with the essentials and avoid the temptation of luxury baby gear that won't make your life—or your baby's—any easier.

MELISSA COX, CFP®

It's no secret that adding children to your family will shake up your budget, and planning ahead is crucial. You'll want to adjust your budget to include:

- **Housing**: Do you need more space for your growing family? That could mean upsizing your home, which comes with its own set of costs—think larger mortgage payments, higher utility bills, and maybe even a little extra for a yard. Let's be real though—babies are small. They don't require a 5,000 square-foot-house with a massive backyard for running around—even if that's something *you* would like. What they really need is a modest, affordable starter home or apartment with geographic access to your support system and a neighborhood with good schools. Plus, a smaller home has another perk—it's easier to clean! Between diaper changes and what feels like 75 loads of laundry a day, you won't want to spend your limited free time cleaning a sprawling house. Sometimes, less space equals less stress. And less stress is priceless on those sleepless nights when even the smallest tasks can feel overwhelming.

- **Healthcare**: Children bring new health expenses—everything from pediatrician visits to vaccinations to endless tubes of diaper cream. It's important to adjust your healthcare budget accordingly and make sure your insurance coverage meets the needs of your growing family.

- **Life Insurance**: Locking in a policy early ensures your family is protected, often at a lower cost. Group life insurance through work is a convenient and affordable option, if you have it. However, consider purchasing an individual policy for additional benefits like portability and, in some cases, long-term care benefits, for the policyholder. This is especially relevant for parents, as it provides financial security for your family if something unexpected happens to you. We will talk more about insurance in subsequent chapters.

Luckily, there are many ways to save money while raising children—especially in the early years. For example, given that children outgrow their clothes faster than you can think, shopping secondhand for gently used items can save you a bundle without sacrificing quality. Facebook and other social media platforms have local groups where parents can trade, sell, or buy kids' clothes, toys, and furniture. It's a great way to pass along things your kids no longer use and snag new items at a low cost. And with a growing family, grocery bills can skyrocket. Meal planning helps you stretch your food budget and avoid the temptation to eat out.

It's also great to talk about money with your children, and the sooner you start teaching them, the better. Use allowances, savings jars, or even apps that teach budgeting skills. The goal is to make sure your children are financially literate by the time they reach adulthood.

### From Conception to Adulthood: Financial Planning for Each Stage

Planning for kids financially isn't just about the early years—it's a long-term commitment that requires flexibility and foresight. Let's walk through a few key stages and how to handle them financially.

MELISSA COX, CFP®

### Stage 1: Before Birth

Financial planning for kids starts before they even arrive. From prenatal care to baby gear, the costs begin long before the baby does. It's helpful to create a baby fund early on. This can be used for medical costs (hello, hospital bills!), nursery setup, and all those adorable baby clothes that you'll use for about three months before they're outgrown. Some tips for preparing your budget during this phase:

- **Know your maternity leave policy**. Before you take time off, make sure you fully understand your employer's maternity and paternity leave policy. How much time are you allowed? Is it paid or unpaid? This can dramatically affect your family's income during those first few months.

- **Weigh the costs of supplemental disability insurance**. If your employer offers a supplemental disability policy, it's worth considering. These policies can help replace a portion of your income while you're on unpaid medical leave and may cover some hospital bills. Just make sure you factor in the cost of the policy versus the benefit.

- **Start saving early**. Even setting aside a small amount each month can help ease the financial burden when the baby arrives.

- **Create a baby registry**. Get financial help from friends and family with essential items.

- **Check your health insurance**: When it comes to prenatal and childbirth expenses, make sure you understand what's covered and what's not.

### Stage 2: Toddler to Elementary

Once your child is born, the financial landscape changes. You're now dealing with the everyday costs of diapers, formula, and early childhood care. If both parents work, finding affordable and reliable childcare will be one of your biggest expenses in these early years. To manage this, consider:

> **Flexible Spending Account (FSA)**
>
> An employer-sponsored, tax-advantaged account that lets employees save pre-tax dollars for eligible healthcare or dependent-care expenses.

- **Childcare tax credits**: Explore tax benefits that help offset the cost of care.

- **Flexible Spending Accounts (FSA)**: If your employer offers one, use an FSA to cover eligible childcare expenses, and remember that all FSA money must be spent by the end of the year.

- **Budgeting for extra activities**: As your child grows, you might start introducing activities like swimming lessons, music classes, and sports or summer camps. These extras can sneak up on you, so build them into your budget early.

- **Future Savings**: You may have just gotten a "raise" by no longer having to pay for childcare if your children go to public school. But instead of increasing your lifestyle, consider redirecting that cash flow into an education fund. This reallocation can help you plan for future tuition or other schooling costs down the road.

### Stage 3: Middle and High School

By the time your child reaches middle school, their costs might start to look a little different—think after-school programs, school trips, and those infamous brand-name clothes.

MELISSA COX, CFP®

Here are a few things to keep in mind during these years:

- **School expenses**: Budget for extracurriculars, field trips, and other school-related activities.
- **Allowance or chores?**: Many parents introduce an allowance at this stage as a way to teach kids about money management. Some tie it to chores, while others use it as a financial learning tool. Either way, it's a great time to introduce financial responsibility.
- **Encouraging part-time jobs**: Whether it's babysitting or mowing lawns, I'm a huge fan of kids earning their own spending money. Not only does this build independence, but it also teaches the value of a dollar—and it helps them appreciate what they spend it on.

### Stage 4: College and Beyond

And then comes college—the financial mountain that looms over every parent. College expenses are daunting, but with some preparation, they don't have to break the bank. Decide and communicate early with your child about how you intend to finance their education. We'll go into college costs in depth in the next chapter. In the meantime, here are a few tips:

> **529 Plan**
>
> 529 Plans are tax-advantaged accounts that can be used to pay for a variety of educational expenses. Each state and DC sponsors its own 529 Plan, and the rules and regulations vary.

- **529 College Savings Plans**: Start saving early with a tax-advantaged

529 plan which allows your money to grow tax-free when used for educational expenses. Some states even match some of what you save; look into what your state offers.

- **Financial aid**: Explore financial aid options, scholarships, and grants to help ease the burden. Complete the FAFSA for need-based financial assistance.
- **Living expenses**: If your child is living away from home, they'll have rent, groceries, and other living expenses. Helping them budget these costs is a great life lesson.
- **Part-time jobs**: Encourage your college student to get a part-time job or to be part of a work/study program. Not only can they help your family by contributing to their living expenses, but when they do this, it also teaches them the value of balancing their work life with their school work. After all, they won't be in class 24/7, and earning their own money builds independence.

*Training Takeaway:*
*The Joys and Frustrations of Parenthood*

Raising children is an incredible adventure filled with equal parts joy and frustration. There will be days when you're bursting with pride at your child's accomplishments, and then there will be days when you're wondering how you became the CEO of a household where socks and sanity mysteriously disappear.

Financially, kids will keep you on your toes—whether it's the endless list of unexpected expenses or the way they outgrow shoes faster than you can say "new pair." But here's the thing: The joy of watching them grow, learn, and become their own little people is priceless. No budget spreadsheet could ever fully capture the love, laughter, and even the chaos that come with raising kids.

So while the costs of parenting are real and sometimes overwhelming, the rewards make it all worth it. In the end, it's all about finding the balance between managing the finances and enjoying the journey. And remember, even on the toughest days, the good moments often outshine the bad.

## College Planning:
## Avoiding the Nightmare of Student-Loan Debt

Let's be honest, college planning isn't what it used to be. Back in the day, attending college could cost no more than a few hundred dollars per year, and students could graduate debt-free with nothing more than a part-time job and maybe a little financial help from their parents.

But today? Well, today we're living in a world where student-loan debt has turned into a full-blown crisis. If there's anything we've learned over the last decade, it's that the way we plan and pay for college is broken.

And here's the kicker—college planning comes at a really awkward time in your family's life. Trust me, I get it (and sorry, mom, I really do understand now). Your teenager is on the verge of independence, emotions are running high, and discussions about finances can quickly turn heated. Everyone's coming into the conversation from a different starting place, and sometimes it feels like you're talking to a brick wall.

But before we let our 18-year-olds make the single biggest investment of their lives, let's try to find some common ground. Cooler heads need to prevail here because this decision will impact your family's finances for years to come.

MELISSA COX, CFP®

The college buying process has become a reactive event. We fall in love with the idea of a school, make our decisions, and then scramble to figure out how we're going to pay for it. But that's the problem—by the time the acceptance letter arrives, the financial conversation feels like an afterthought, and suddenly families are staring down the barrel of tuition bills they weren't prepared for. We've got it backward.

### Reactive vs. Proactive: Changing the Way We Plan for College

The key to turning this process around is making it proactive. College planning should start with a budget, not with campus tours. Before your family even steps foot on a college campus, you need to run the numbers.

What's realistic for your family? What does the Department of Education expect you to contribute based on your income and assets, also known as your Student Aid Index (SAI)? These are the conversations that need to happen long before your kid picks their "dream school."

Too often, we're reactive instead of proactive, falling in love with a school and then trying to figure out how to pay for it. If you've ever tried to discuss your budget after a campus tour

**The Student Aid Index (SAI)**

The SAI is a formula-based index schools use to determine how much financial support a student may need. It is calculated based on information provided in the federal Free Application for Federal Student Aid (FAFSA®) form.

involving luxury dorms and lazy rivers, you know how difficult this can be. (Yes, *lazy rivers*—seriously!)

So let's change the conversation before the dream school takes over. Proactive planning can mean the difference between a manageable investment and a financial burden that lasts decades.

### The Importance of a College Budget

It might not be the most exciting part of the process, but creating a college budget is essential. Think of it as your financial road map to make

> College planning should start with a budget, not with campus tours. Before your family even steps foot on a college campus, you need to run the numbers.

sure you can afford college without derailing your retirement plans, because trust me, no one wants to be paying for both at the same time.

Planning for college should ideally begin in the summer before your kids enter high school. Why? Because soon after that, your family's income alone will set the tone for what you'll be expected to pay for college. Your income is the biggest factor in the SAI, and unfortunately, shifting assets around won't make much of a difference if you're already considered a "full pay" family based on your income.

Once you have an idea of your financial landscape, you can

start setting boundaries for your college search. And yes, these conversations need to involve your child. They need to understand the financial side of education before you start visiting campuses.

The FAFSA (Free Application for Federal Student Aid) Forecaster tool can give you a heads-up on what colleges will likely expect you to contribute. If you're new to this, get ready—FAFSA is about to become a very familiar part of your life. (And yes, parents everywhere rejoice when they no longer have to deal with it!)

Knowing that your income will be a major factor in financial aid calculations, the Forecaster helps you build a realistic budget and adjust your financial strategy early. By the time your child is filling out applications, you'll be ready to have that all-important conversation about what's affordable and what's not.

### Know Your Student, Know Your Schools

Once you've got a budget in place, the next step is school selection. Be careful—this is where a lot of families make mistakes. It's not just about finding the best academic fit—it's also about finding the right financial fit. There are schools out there that cater to students with high financial need and others that offer significant merit-based scholarships, but you have to know what you're looking for.

For example, if your student is looking for a merit-based scholarship, schools like MIT or Harvard might not be the best choice. Why? Because at these top-tier institutions, most students are at the top of their game. In fact, Ivy League schools and similarly competitive universities don't generally offer merit-based scholarships—they simply don't need to, as they could fill their entire freshman class with valedictorians if they wanted to.

On the other hand, many schools actively seek standout students and may offer generous financial-aid packages, including merit-based scholarships, to make attending more possible. This is where understanding your student's academic strengths, needs, and potential for merit aid comes into play.

### State Schools vs. Private Schools: The Real Cost

When it comes to choosing between state schools and private schools, there's a common misconception that state schools are always the less expensive option.

It seems logical—state schools are publicly funded, so they should be the most affordable, right? Well, not necessarily. Here's where families can get tripped up—sticker prices don't tell the whole story.

The truth is that state schools often have limited financial resources when it comes to offering financial aid. Private schools, on the other hand, frequently have large endowments. That gives them more flexibility to make the school more affordable and attract students who might otherwise be scared off by the sticker price.

Take time to run the numbers, and you might be surprised at what you find. Focus on the net cost of attendance—that's what really matters. This can include everything from room and board to fees and extras, and, of course, any financial aid that reduces the overall price tag.

MELISSA COX, CFP®

## Understanding Early Action and Early Decision

When it comes to applying to college, many schools offer two options: Early Action and Early Decision. While both let you apply early, they come with different commitments.

Early Action allows you to apply early without the commitment to attend, giving you more flexibility to compare financial-aid offers from a variety of schools.

Early Decision, however, is binding. If you apply Early Decision and you're accepted, you have committed to attend that school—often before knowing your full financial-aid package. That can lock you into a full pay situation, regardless of what your FAFSA might determine.

Even if the financial-aid package isn't as generous as hoped, you're still obligated to attend—making it a riskier option for families depending on aid. Carefully consider your family's financial situation before allowing your student to apply Early Decision. While it might boost the chance of acceptance, it's important to ensure you're financially prepared to meet the potential cost.

## The Value of Waiting for Financial Aid Packages

Patience is key when it comes to finalizing your college decision. Waiting for all your student's financial aid packages to arrive can provide valuable leverage. Once you have the offers in hand, you may even be able to use them as bargaining chips to negotiate for more aid. Schools are sometimes willing to increase their offer if they know applicants received a better package elsewhere.

Just don't rush to commit too early. That dream offer might

be just around the corner sitting in a large envelope, making the wait worth it!

### The Value of AP Courses, Dual-Credit Programs, and Community Colleges

One of the smartest ways to reduce the overall cost of college is by earning credits before you even step foot on campus. AP courses, dual-credit programs, and local community colleges can be a game changer in this regard, offering students a head start on their education without the hefty price tag.

Advanced Placement (AP) courses and dual-credit programs allow high school students to earn college credits while still in high school. Not only do these programs challenge students academically but they also can significantly reduce the amount of time and money spent in college. Think about it—if your student can knock out a semester or even a year's worth of credits while still in high school, they're saving thousands of dollars in tuition, room, and board.

AP courses offer college-level curricula and the chance to earn college credit by scoring well on the AP exams. Dual-credit programs, on the other hand, allow students to take actual college courses, often through partnerships with local community colleges or universities, and earn both high school and college credit simultaneously.

Local community colleges also provide an excellent and often underappreciated option for cutting college costs. Community colleges typically have much lower tuition rates than four-year universities, and many offer programs that allow students to complete their first two years of coursework before transferring to a four-year institution.

MELISSA COX, CFP®

As a proud alum of the Dallas County Community College District (now called Dallas College), I can personally attest to the benefits of this path. Not only did attending community college save me money, but it also allowed me to transition into the college experience without any major setbacks. Community colleges offer a smoother, more affordable entry into higher education, making it a great option for students who want to adjust to college life before diving into a four-year university.

## Not Every Path Leads to a Four-Year College— And That's Okay

Let's get real for a minute: A four-year college or university isn't for everyone. And that's perfectly okay. The reality is, not every student is cut out for traditional higher education, and there's no point in wasting thousands of dollars only to have your child "find themselves on a lifelong sabbatical in a remote village in South America" after graduation—unless, of course, that's exactly where they want to be, and they've done the work to fund it and can stay off their parent's payroll.

The beauty of this world is that we need people doing all sorts of jobs. Trade schools, apprenticeships, and vocational training programs are fantastic alternatives for students who aren't quite ready for—nor interested in—college life. These paths offer valuable skills, great job prospects, and the chance to start a career without racking up a mountain of debt.

At the end of the day, what really matters isn't whether your child has a degree from a fancy university. What matters is that your child is off the parental payroll and is living a life that brings them purpose and fulfillment.

And honestly, the quality that matters most is kindness. A kind young adult who is independent and contributes to society in a way that suits them—that's the ultimate success story.

## Training Takeaway: Proactive College Planning

College is one of the biggest financial decisions your family will make, and it's time to stop treating it like an afterthought. Instead of reacting to acceptance letters and scrambling to figure out how to pay for it, let's flip the script and be proactive.

Start with a budget. Have the tough conversations about money early on. Involve your kids in the financial decision-making process so they understand the impact their college choice will have on both their future and yours. And most importantly, remember that this decision isn't just about the next four years—it's about setting everyone up for success long after graduation.

MELISSA Cox, CFP®

# What You Can and Cannot Control in Retirement, and Where You Have Partial Control

Retirement planning is about managing what you can, preparing for what you can't, and making the best possible decisions in those areas where you have partial control. Understanding the differences between these categories is key to building a retirement plan that's flexible, resilient, and tailored to your unique situation.

There's no way around it—retirement planning can be stressful. I've had many clients come to me feeling overwhelmed, thinking they need to control every single detail of their retirement to ensure a perfect, stress-free future. They want certainty over how long their money will last, how long they'll live, what healthcare will cost, and even what the stock market will do from year to year.

But here's the reality: Trying to control every single aspect of retirement is not only impossible, it's also exhausting. The truth is, no matter how well you plan, some things will always be out of your hands.

The key is to avoid obsessing over the uncontrollable and to focus on what *you can* manage while preparing for the unexpected as best as you can.

## What You Can Control in Retirement

- **Your Savings Rate.** One of the most powerful things you can control when planning for retirement is how much you save. The earlier you start saving and the more consistent you are, the more prepared you'll be when retirement comes around. Take advantage of employer-sponsored retirement plans, individual retirement accounts (IRAs), and tax-efficient saving strategies to boost your contributions. If you are self-employed, options like SEP IRAs or solo 401(k)s can help you achieve similar goals. We'll cover these types of accounts and how to use them in detail in an upcoming chapter, so stay tuned!

> Retirement planning is about managing what you can, preparing for what you can't, making the best possible decisions in those areas where you have partial control—and understanding the differences between these categories.

- **Your Spending Habits.** Your spending habits in retirement will have a direct impact on how long your savings last. While it's tempting to splurge in the early years, being mindful of your expenses can help you enjoy retirement without

MELISSA COX, CFP®

> **Required Minimum Distribution (RMD)**
>
> The amount of money that must be withdrawn annually by retirees of a specified age from certain retirement plans including 401(k)s and traditional IRAs.

financial stress. Create a realistic retirement budget that accounts for essentials like housing, healthcare, and discretionary spending, and regularly adjust it to reflect your evolving lifestyle.

- **Your Investment Strategy.** The way you manage your investments during retirement is crucial to maintaining your financial health. While market performance is unpredictable, your investment choices can help manage risk and maximize growth. Ensure your portfolio is diversified and aligned with your risk tolerance, especially as you transition from accumulation to preservation in retirement.

- **When You Retire.** While you may dream of retiring at 60, delaying retirement by even a few years can significantly boost your financial security. Working longer allows you to save more, grow your investments, and increase your Social Security benefits. If possible, consider delaying retirement to maximize benefits and ensure a more comfortable lifestyle throughout your retirement years.

- **Your Withdrawal Strategy.** How much and when you withdraw from your retirement accounts is a decision that's entirely in your hands. A strategic withdrawal plan can help you manage taxes, avoid penalties, and make your savings last longer. Work with a financial planner to create a tax-efficient withdrawal plan, considering factors like Required

Minimum Distributions (RMDs) and timing your withdrawals for the lowest tax impact.

### What You Cannot Control in Retirement

- **Longevity.** No one knows exactly how long they'll live, which makes retirement planning tricky. While living a long life is a blessing, it also means your savings need to last longer than you might have anticipated. Plan for a longer retirement than you expect. Assume you'll live into your 90s, even if that feels overly cautious. Life insurance or annuities can provide additional income security if you're concerned about outliving your savings.

- **Market Performance.** No matter how well you plan, the stock market can—and will—go through periods of volatility. While you can control your investment strategy, you can't predict how the markets will perform year to year. Build a diversified portfolio that can weather market downturns, and avoid panic-selling during periods of volatility. Stay focused on long-term goals rather than on short-term fluctuations.

- **Healthcare.** The cost of healthcare is one of the biggest unknowns in retirement. Medical expenses, long-term care, and insurance premiums are rising, and it's hard to predict exactly how much you'll need to cover them. Consider purchasing long-term care insurance or setting aside a portion of your savings specifically for healthcare costs. If you are eligible, it's also worth maximizing Health Savings Accounts (HSAs) while you are working.

MELISSA COX, CFP®

- **Inflation.** Inflation erodes your purchasing power over time, meaning the cost of living will likely increase throughout your retirement. While you can't control inflation, you can build a plan that accounts for it. Make sure your investment portfolio includes assets like stocks, real estate, or inflation-protected securities (such as Treasury Inflation-Protected Securities also known as TIPS) that can help protect your savings from the effects of inflation.
- **Tax Policy Changes**. Tax laws change over time, and while you can make strategic tax decisions today, you can't predict how future policy changes might affect your retirement withdrawals or income. Focus on building a tax-diversified portfolio by utilizing different types of accounts (like Roth IRAs, traditional IRAs, and taxable brokerage accounts) to give yourself flexibility no matter what future tax policy changes may occur.

### *What You Have Some Control Over in Retirement*

Here's where things get a little more nuanced. Some factors that influence your retirement aren't entirely out of your hands, but neither are they 100% under your control. These are areas where you can make decisions to influence the outcome, but external factors still play a role.
- **Longevity.** While you can't fully control how long you live, your lifestyle choices—like diet, exercise, and healthcare—can certainly impact your longevity. However, genetics and unforeseen medical issues are always wildcards. Take care of your health by maintaining an active lifestyle, eating well, and staying on top of preventive healthcare. While you can't change your genetic makeup, living a healthy life can

increase your chances for a longer, healthier retirement.

- **Employment and Earning Duration.** While you can't entirely predict how long you'll be able to work or whether job opportunities will continue as you age, you do have some say in how long you stay in the workforce. Factors like job satisfaction, career choices, and upskilling

## Roth IRA

A retirement account funded with after-tax dollars, where investments grow tax-free and withdrawals are tax-free in retirement.

## Traditional IRA

A retirement account where contributions may be tax-deductible, but withdrawals in retirement are taxed as ordinary income.

can influence whether you continue working past the traditional retirement age. Focus on staying relevant in your career by continuing to learn and upskill. If you're in a career that's physically demanding, consider transitioning to work that's less strenuous but still keeps you engaged and earning. You can also explore part-time or freelance work in retirement to extend your earning years. However, keep in mind that unexpected factors like layoffs, health issues, or changes in the economy could impact your ability to continue working for as long as you'd like.

- **Healthcare.** While you can't control how much healthcare costs will rise, you can take proactive steps to manage healthcare-related expenses. Planning for long-term care, using health savings accounts (HSAs) and choosing appropriate Medicare plans are within your control, but the overall cost

MELISSA COX, CFP®

structure of the healthcare system isn't. Consider purchasing long-term care insurance or setting aside extra funds to cover healthcare in retirement. As previously mentioned, max out your HSA contributions if you're eligible as this will give you a tax-advantaged way to pay for medical expenses down the road.

- **Social Security Benefits.** While you can't change the rules of Social Security, you do have control over when you start claiming your benefits. Delaying Social Security until full retirement age (or beyond) can significantly increase your monthly payments. If you are in good health, it may be wise to wait until full retirement age—or even until 70—to claim your Social Security benefits. This is one area where your decision-making can have a big impact on your retirement income.

### Training Takeaway

Here's the bottom line: Focus your energy on what you *can* control, like your savings rate and spending habits. Stay mindful of the factors you *can't* control, like tax policy or longevity, and prepare for uncertainty as best as you can. And in those areas where you have *some* control—like healthcare costs or your working years—make informed decisions that will give you more flexibility in retirement.

By keeping this balance in mind, you can create a retirement plan that's realistic, sustainable, and adaptable to whatever comes your way.

# Estate Planning and Wealth Transfer: Protecting Your Legacy

When people think about financial planning, the usual suspects come to mind—saving for retirement, investing wisely, and managing debt. But one of the most overlooked (yet crucial) aspects is estate planning. It's easy to think estate planning is only for the ultra-wealthy, but the reality is, no matter the size of your estate, this step is key to protecting your legacy. Estate planning isn't just about money—it's also about making sure your assets and values are passed down in line with your wishes.

Without a proper estate plan, the wealth you've worked so hard to build could be left in legal limbo—or worse, end up in the wrong hands.

And by "wrong hands," I mean your ex-spouse getting your prized assets, which would make for a *great* episode of *Real Housewives*. Oh, they would enjoy it, but that's the *last* thing you'd want to happen. While it might not be the most exciting part of financial planning, estate planning is absolutely essential to safeguarding everything you've built.

MELISSA COX, CFP®

Estate planning isn't just about dividing up assets after you're gone. It also ensures that your loved ones are cared for, that your wealth is protected, and that your wishes are honored. Here's why estate planning should be a priority for everyone:

- **Protecting Your Family.** An estate plan ensures your loved ones are taken care of after you're gone. If you have minor children, it allows you to designate a guardian ensuring their care and financial well-being. For adult dependents, estate planning helps them access the financial resources they need to maintain their lifestyle.

- **Avoiding Probate.** Dying without an estate plan or will means your estate goes through probate, a legal process that can be time-consuming, expensive, and stressful for your family. Proper estate planning allows you to avoid probate, ensuring your assets are distributed efficiently and end up where *you* intend them to go.

- **Minimizing Taxes.** By using other financial planning or asset gifting methods, you can maximize the finances passed on to your loved ones and reduce estate taxes.

- **Honoring Your Wishes.** Without an estate plan, state laws determine how your assets are distributed through the probate process. This could lead to outcomes that don't align with your wishes. Estate planning gives you control, ensuring your assets are divided according to your personal and family values.

### Essential Estate Planning Documents: What You Need

A solid estate plan relies on a few key documents to ensure your wishes are carried out and your family is protected. The essential documents that form the backbone of your estate plan are:

- **Wills.** A will outlines how you want your assets to be distributed after your death, who will manage your estate—your executor(s)—and who will serve as a guardian for any minor children.
- **Medical Directives.** A medical directive (or living will) provides instructions for your healthcare if you become incapacitated and are unable to communicate your wishes. It covers decisions such as life support, resuscitation, and other medical treatments, ensuring that your healthcare preferences are honored without putting the burden of difficult decisions on family members.
- **Powers of Attorney.** A power of attorney designates someone to handle your financial matters if you're unable to do so. This person can make decisions, pay bills, and manage your financial affairs. You'll also want a healthcare power of attorney giving someone the authority to make medical decisions on your behalf if necessary. You can designate the same person for both roles or choose two different individuals depending on your preferences and needs.

It's important to note that if you have both a medical directive and a healthcare power of attorney, the medical

> Estate planning should be a priority for everyone. It ensures that your loved ones are cared for, that your wealth is protected, and that your wishes are honored.

MELISSA COX, CFP®

directive typically takes precedence. The person holding your healthcare power of attorney is generally expected to follow the instructions in your medical directive, ensuring that your specific healthcare wishes are respected. However, if any situations arise that aren't directly addressed in your medical directive, your healthcare power of attorney will then have the authority to make decisions based on what they believe aligns with your preferences.

### Trusts: A Key Tool in Estate Planning

Trusts are one of the most powerful tools in estate planning, allowing you to protect and distribute your assets efficiently while avoiding probate. Trusts come in various forms, but here are three of the most common:

- **Revocable Living Trust.** A revocable living trust allows you to control your assets during your lifetime and designate how they should be distributed after your death. One of the major benefits of this type of trust is that it avoids probate. It's also flexible, allowing you to modify or revoke it during your lifetime.
- **Irrevocable Trust.** Unlike a revocable trust, an irrevocable trust removes assets from your estate entirely. Once set up, it cannot be changed, but this offers significant advantages such as minimizing estate taxes and protecting assets from creditors. By reducing the taxable value of your estate, an irrevocable trust can help lower the tax burden on your heirs.
- **Charitable Trusts:** Charitable trusts, such as a charitable remainder trust, allow you to leave a portion of your estate to a nonprofit organization. This strategy can reduce the taxable value of your estate while supporting causes

you care about. It's a way to make a meaningful impact and enjoy potential tax benefits at the same time.

### Strategies for Minimizing Estate Taxes

Minimizing estate taxes is often a top concern for those with larger estates. While you will need to work with a tax attorney on your particular estate, here are two commonly-used strategies to reduce the impact of taxes on your estate:

- **Gifting During Your Lifetime.** The IRS allows you to gift a certain amount of money each year ($19,000 per recipient at the time of this writing) without triggering a gift tax. Over time, these gifts can significantly reduce the size of your taxable estate, lowering the potential tax burden on your heirs.
- **Charitable Giving.** Leaving a portion of your estate to a qualified charitable nonprofit can reduce the taxable value of your estate while supporting causes you care about. A charitable remainder trust is one way to accomplish this, allowing you to make a difference while minimizing estate taxes.

### An Estate Planning Attorney or an Online Service?

With the rise of online legal packages, you may wonder whether you really need an estate planning attorney or if a DIY solution is good enough. While online services may seem convenient, estate planning isn't something you want to take lightly—especially if your financial situation is complex. Here are some points to consider:

Estate planning attorneys offer expertise and personalized

advice helping you avoid costly mistakes. They'll work with you to craft an estate plan tailored to your family's unique needs and ensure your documents are legally sound. This is especially critical for those with complex estates or specific asset-protection goals.

For those with simpler financial situations, online estate planning packages can be a cost-effective option. However, these solutions may not account for all the nuances of state law or your unique family dynamics. If you do opt for an online package, it's worth having a professional review the documents to ensure there are no gaps.

It's worth checking to see whether your employer offers estate planning benefits. Many companies now provide access to legal services as part of their benefits package, making it easier (and more affordable) to complete essential documents like wills, trusts, and powers of attorney. If you have access to these services, take advantage of them—they can significantly reduce the cost of estate planning.

### Passing on Financial Values and Principles

Estate planning isn't just about transferring wealth. It's also about passing on your values, principles, and financial wisdom. After all, leaving an inheritance is only meaningful if your heirs know how to manage it responsibly.

Start talking to your family about your estate plan, your financial journey, and the values that have guided your decisions. This transparency can help avoid confusion later and ensure your heirs are prepared to manage what they inherit.

One of the greatest gifts you can give your heirs is a financial education. Make sure they understand the basics of managing money, including budgeting, investing, and planning for the future. Consider holding regular family meetings to discuss the estate plan and broader financial goals. This helps set clear expectations and promotes family harmony, preventing disputes down the road.

## Training Takeaway: Securing Your Legacy

Estate planning is about more than just ensuring your assets end up in the right hands—it's also about preserving your legacy and protecting the people and values you care about most. Whether your estate is large or small, proper planning can minimize taxes, avoid probate, and ensure that your wishes are honored. By taking action now, you're setting your family up for success long after you're gone.

And remember, estate planning isn't a one-and-done task. As your financial situation, family, and priorities change, so should your estate plan. Regularly reviewing and updating your plan ensures that it continues to reflect your goals and secures the legacy you want to leave behind.

MELISSA COX, CFP®

# Multigenerational Financial Planning: Setting Up Your Legacy for the Long Haul

Let's talk about the big picture—the really big picture. You've worked hard to build a solid financial foundation, but what happens next? What's the long-term goal beyond your own financial security? For many, the answer is setting up future generations for success. Enter multigenerational financial planning: It's not just about securing your future; it's also about creating a legacy that benefits your children, grandchildren, and beyond. (Cue future family reunions where your name gets mentioned in awe for that smart planning you did back in the day.)

Here's the thing—you don't need to be a millionaire to start thinking about multigenerational planning. With a solid plan, a long-term perspective, and smart financial decisions, you can build a legacy that lasts generations.

## What is Multigenerational Financial Planning?

At its core, multigenerational financial planning is about more than just estate planning—it's also about creating a legacy that includes both tangible assets and the financial values that underpin them. While estate planning focuses on the mechanics of distributing your wealth and minimizing taxes after your lifetime, multigenerational planning takes a broader approach. It emphasizes preparing your heirs to manage and grow the assets they inherit, ensuring your legacy extends beyond money to include principles, strategies, and a long-term vision. This approach equips future generations not just with financial support for milestones like college, homeownership, or retirement, but also with the tools to sustain and build upon that foundation.

The earlier you begin, the easier it is to build systems that benefit your family long after you're gone. It's not just about creating wealth but also about ensuring that the next generation knows how to manage it.

## Family Office Management: Organizing and Growing Family Wealth

When it comes to handling wealth across generations, the concept of family office management becomes important. And it's not as complicated as it sounds. Family office management refers to a structured way of handling your finances and ensuring that assets continue to grow and are distributed efficiently over time.

A family office could range from a full team of financial professionals, accountants, and attorneys, to something simpler, like a clear system for managing investments and wealth. The goal is to have your assets protected, growing, and passed down according to your wishes. It's about ensuring that everything is organized so your family knows where your import-

MELISSA COX, CFP®

ant documents are and that your wealth doesn't disappear into thin air because someone forgot a password.

### Key People in Your Financial Plan: Beneficiaries

Beneficiary designations are one of the simplest ways to ensure your assets go directly to the people you choose—no probate, no fuss. Accounts like IRAs, retirement plans, and life insurance policies allow you to name beneficiaries, so your assets pass directly to them when you're gone. Easy, right?

Not so fast. If you haven't updated those beneficiary designations in a while, they might not reflect your current wishes. (You don't want an ex-spouse getting your 401(k), do you?) Keep these updated, especially after major life events like marriage, divorce, or the birth of a child.

But here's something you should know: Inheriting certain assets, like an IRA, comes with its own set of rules, particularly the 10-year rule introduced in 2020.

Before 2020, beneficiaries could "stretch" distributions from inherited IRAs over their lifetimes, allowing for tax-deferred growth. However, with the new 10-year rule, non-spouse beneficiaries now have 10 years to withdraw the entire balance. This may seem like plenty of time, but it creates challenges. For one, it can throw your beneficiary into a higher tax bracket, resulting in an unexpected tax burden.

For example, let's say your adult child inherits your IRA while they're in their prime earning years. They might already be in a high tax bracket, and adding large withdrawals from the IRA could lead to an even bigger tax bill. They may also be tempted to spend the money quickly, not realizing that they're sacrificing long-term growth.

Depending on the stage of life the beneficiary is in, without a plan, inheriting a large pool of money can do more harm than good. And let's face it, even the best of us are tempted when there's a big pot of money sitting in front of us.

## Understanding the Impact of Inherited Wealth

It's important to think about how inheriting a large sum at different life stages could impact your beneficiaries:

### In Their 20s or 30s.

Let's be honest—most people in their 20s or early 30s aren't known for stellar financial decision-making. (Remember when we thought Beanie Babies were a good investment?) If a young beneficiary inherits a large IRA, they might spend it too quickly without realizing the long-term consequences, potentially losing out on decades of growth.

### In Their 40s or 50s.

For someone in their prime earning years, inheriting an IRA might seem like a financial windfall. But with the 10-year rule, they could be looking at a massive tax hit, especially if they're already in a high tax bracket. Without careful planning, this could chip away at the inheritance and even create unexpected financial stress.

Beyond the tax implications, inheriting a large sum of money could also impact the cost of paying for a child's education. Here's why: The increase in taxable income from IRA withdrawals might raise the family's Student Aid Index when applying for financial aid.

Colleges look at a family's income and assets to determine

MELISSA COX, CFP®

how much financial aid they qualify for. A higher SAI could mean less financial aid and more out-of-pocket costs for tuition, making it even more important to carefully plan how and when withdrawals are made.

Without a solid plan, this unexpected windfall could make the cost of college rise at a time when a family is already balancing multiple financial priorities.

To address this potential liability, work with a financial professional to understand how an inheritance or other windfall might affect your Student Aid Index (SAI). This can help you strategize how to allocate or shelter funds to minimize the impact on financial aid eligibility.

If possible, time the receipt or use of inherited funds strategically. For example, paying down debts or making qualified contributions to retirement accounts before filling out the FAFSA could help lower your reported assets.

Depending on your financial situation, consider options like funding 529 plans or other tax-advantaged accounts to reduce taxable income and to ensure the windfall is allocated for future educational needs.

Adjust your financial plans and budget to accommodate the impact of the windfall while maintaining a balance between current needs and future goals, including college expenses.

By taking these steps, you can effectively manage the impact of an unexpected inheritance or windfall, ensuring it aligns with your overall financial priorities and supports—not hinders—your family's educational goals.

### Near Retirement.

For older beneficiaries, inheriting an IRA could provide much-needed retirement income. But with the compressed

10-year window for withdrawals, they need to be careful about how they take the money to avoid triggering higher taxes.

## Key People in Your Financial Plan: Executor(s)

Your executor is responsible for carrying out your will and managing your estate after you're gone. They'll handle everything from distributing assets to settling debts and navigating the legal process. So it's important to choose someone who not only understands your wishes but is also capable of making tough decisions.

This is not a job for just anyone. It's a serious responsibility, and picking the right person can make all the difference in how smoothly things go after you're gone. If you have a complex estate or if family dynamics are tricky, consider appointing a professional or corporate trustee to handle these responsibilities.

## Trusts and Life Insurance: Protecting Generational Wealth

Trusts and life insurance are essential tools for managing and protecting multigenerational wealth. While trusts allow you to control how and when your assets are distributed, life insurance can offer a financial safety net, providing liquidity and ensuring that your beneficiaries are protected financially when you pass away.

Trusts are legal entities that manage how your wealth is distributed to beneficiaries, shielding assets from taxes, creditors, and even poor financial decisions by your heirs.

Beyond just providing a payout, life insurance can be used strategically to create cash value, ensuring that your loved ones have the liquidity they need when they need it.

Both tools are designed to protect your wealth and ensure it's distributed in a way that reflects your wishes. Better yet, neither are affected by that pesky 10-year rule.

### Specific Benefits of Family Office Management

As we said earlier, the concept of the Family Office Management is simple: to organize your family's wealth in a way that ensures it continues to grow and is distributed effectively over time. You don't need a massive fortune to benefit from family office principles. Whether you hire professionals or manage it yourself, the key is having a clear plan in place.

A family office helps you:

- **Centralize financial records**. You can keep everything from tax returns to estate documents in one place.
- **Coordinate with professionals.** You will work with financial planners, estate attorneys, and accountants to make sure everything runs smoothly.
- **Create family meetings**: Holding regular discussions about financial goals, estate plans, and legacy will help prevent disputes and confusion later on.

### Educating the Next Generation

As the saying goes, "Give someone a fish, and they'll eat for a day; teach them to fish, and they'll eat for a lifetime." The same idea applies to generational wealth. It's not just about leaving behind money—it's also about passing on the knowledge to manage it wisely. By teaching your heirs how to handle finances, you're giving them the skills they need to sustain and grow that wealth for years to come.

There are many ways to teach financial literacy, including:

- **Money management basics**. Budgeting, saving, and understanding debt are all essential.
- **Investment education**. Help them understand how investments work and why long-term growth matters.
- **Involving them early**. Involve your family in financial discussions and decisions so they understand your goals and can continue the legacy.

### Training Takeaway: Creating a Lasting Legacy

Remember, *it's your race, your pace*. Setting up a lasting legacy takes time and thoughtful planning, but with the right approach, you can create a financial future that benefits your family for years to come.

# Our Favorite Uncle Sam:
## Understanding Income Taxes

When I was a child, I asked my younger sister who Uncle Sam was, and she confidently replied, "Oh, he's the guy who points at you and says, 'I want you.'"

While that's not exactly accurate when it comes to taxes, it's an answer that still makes me smile every year as tax season rolls around. Somehow, those memories bubble up every time I see Uncle Sam and Lady Liberty costumes waving tax prep signs on the streets as if they're personally inviting us all to settle up.

Let's be honest: No one *really* looks forward to tax season. It's like that friend who only shows up once a year, but instead of bringing gifts, they bring a pile of forms and a list of things they want from you. And while income taxes might not be anyone's favorite part of financial planning, understanding them is crucial to keeping your finances in check.

Now, taxes aren't all bad. After all, they're part of what keeps our roads paved, our schools running, and Uncle Sam satisfied. But they can still feel like a burden—especially when you're staring down a maze of W-2s, 1099s, and that looming

April 15th deadline. So let's break down the basics and figure out how to make tax season a little more manageable.

### Why Tax Codes Exist and Who Creates Them?

Just when you think you have the tax system figured out, a new rule pops up, and suddenly, you're back to square one. So why does the tax code seem to change so frequently?

The answer lies in the fact that taxes aren't just about collecting money. The tax code is designed to reflect economic policy, incentivize certain behaviors (like saving for retirement), and redistribute wealth to fund public services like education, defense, infrastructure, healthcare, and more. It's a giant balancing act—making sure the government has enough revenue without overburdening taxpayers.

Who creates these tax laws? Congress does, primarily through the House Ways and Means Committee and the Senate Finance Committee. These committees are responsible for proposing changes to the tax code, which are then voted on by Congress and signed into law by the President. This process can be influenced by everything from economic trends to political priorities, affecting the tax code over time.

While tax laws can feel overwhelming, the purpose is to create a system that meets the country's financial needs. However, the constant tweaks and updates can make it difficult to keep up with it, even if you think you've mastered your taxes one year. The best advice? Stay informed and flexible, because when it comes to taxes, change is one of the few constants.

### Income Taxes 101: How It Works

Let's start with the basics. When you earn money, a portion

MELISSA COX, CFP®

> The tax code is designed to reflect economic policy, incentivize certain behaviors (like saving for retirement), and redistribute wealth to fund public services like education, defense, infrastructure, healthcare, and more.

of it goes to the government in the form of income tax. In the United States, this tax is progressive, meaning the more you earn, the higher the percentage of your income you'll pay in taxes. But here's the kicker: Tax brackets aren't quite as straightforward as they look on paper.

For example, if you're in the 24% tax bracket, that doesn't mean you pay 24% of all your income to Uncle Sam. Instead, you pay 10% on the first portion of your income, 12% on the next portion, and so on—and the IRS adjusts the amount of these portions each year. By the time you get to the 24% bracket, you're only paying that rate on a small portion of your total income.

Understanding tax brackets can save you from the common misconception that earning more automatically means you'll lose a big chunk of your paycheck to taxes.

### Deductions and Credits: The Good News

Here's where things get a little better. Deductions and tax credits reduce the amount of income you pay taxes on, but in different ways.

Deductions reduce your taxable income. Common deductions include charitable donations (for amounts above a certain threshold if you itemize deductions), mortgage interest, and contributions to retirement accounts like a 401(k) or IRA.

Tax credits are even better. They directly reduce the amount of tax you owe. For example, the Child Tax Credit or the Earned Income Tax Credit can lower your tax bill significantly.

The key is to understand what deductions and credits you're eligible for and to make sure you're taking advantage of them. For example, if you're contributing to a retirement plan, you're not just saving for your future—you're also reducing your taxable income today. It's a win-win situation.

### Above-the-Line vs. Below-the-Line Deductions: What's the Difference?

When you hear people talking about above-the-line and below-the-line deductions, it's easy to get lost in the jargon. But it's actually simpler than it sounds—and yes, one type of deduction can often be more effective than the other.

Above-the-line deductions reduce your adjusted gross income (AGI) directly. AGI is one of the most important numbers on your tax return because it's used to calculate your tax liability and determine your eligibility for other tax breaks. The more you can lower your AGI, the better. Common examples of

**Adjusted Gross Income (AGI)**

Total income minus certain deductions, serving as the basis for calculating taxable income.

above-the-line deductions include contributions to traditional IRAs, student loan interest, health savings accounts(HSAs), and self-employment expenses. These deductions can be taken even if you don't itemize your taxes.

Below-the-line deductions come into play after you've calculated your AGI and are sometimes referred to as itemized deductions. These include things like mortgage interest, charitable donations (above a certain threshold of your income if you itemize), and medical expenses (exceeding 7.5% of your AGI). You can only take below-the-line deductions if they exceed the standard deduction ($13,850 for individuals and $27,700 for married couples filing jointly in 2023). Otherwise, you'll simply take the standard deduction.

Which is more effective? Generally, above-the-line deductions are more valuable because they lower your AGI, which can impact your tax bracket and make you eligible for other tax credits or deductions. Below-the-line deductions can still be beneficial, especially if you itemize, but above-the-line deductions affect more areas of your tax situation. So if you're deciding where to put your focus, start with those above-the-line opportunities to reduce your AGI.

### The Pitfalls of Avoiding Taxes Completely

No one *likes* paying taxes. In fact, some people take pride in keeping their taxes as low as possible. There's always that friend or colleague who brags about paying next to nothing in taxes. But here's the thing: Completely avoiding taxes isn't always the best financial strategy, especially in the long run.

For starters, Social Security benefits are based on your adjusted gross income and your taxable earnings over your lifetime. If you're not reporting enough income to the IRS, you could be underreporting your earnings for Social Security as well. That means fewer benefits for you when you retire, potentially making life a lot harder in your older years.

It's important to remember that Social Security was never designed to be a stand-alone retirement plan. It was meant to supplement other forms of retirement savings. However, for many Americans, Social Security remains a significant part of their retirement income. If you're not earning enough to qualify for decent Social Security benefits, or if you've neglected to contribute to retirement savings like a 401(k) or IRA, you could be setting yourself up for a financially shaky retirement.

The bottom line is that while minimizing your taxes is a smart strategy, going too far and avoiding them altogether can backfire. You need to think about your future, especially when it comes to Social Security and retirement savings. Pay your fair share now so you don't find yourself scrambling later.

### What's With All These Forms?

Tax season brings with it a barrage of forms. From W-2s to 1099s, these forms tell the IRS how much you earned, how much tax you've already paid, and what you might still owe:

- **W-2.** If you're an employee, your employer will send you this form showing how much you earned and how much tax they withheld on your behalf.

- **1099.** If you're self-employed or an independent contractor, you'll get this form for various types of income, like freelance work, investments, or even gambling winnings.

- **1040.** This is the form you'll fill out (or your accountant will fill out) to calculate your total taxes due. It's where the

MELISSA COX, CFP®

magic—or frustration—happens.

- **1040EZ.** If you have a simple tax situation—think single filer, no dependents, and straightforward income—you may qualify to file this streamlined form.
- **Schedule C.** For those who are self-employed, this is where you list your business income and expenses. It can be both tedious and eye-opening—you might not realize how much you spent on coffee for "business meetings" until you see it all in black and white.

With these forms in hand, you'll be ready to tackle tax season (or hand them off to your accountant) with a clearer understanding of what each one represents.

### Small Businesses and Taxes: What You Need to Know

Speaking of Schedule Cs…If you're a small business owner or self-employed, taxes are a whole different ball game. Running your own business comes with its own set of tax responsibilities, and while there are benefits, there are also a few traps to watch out for. Here's a breakdown of what small business owners need to know:

- **Self-Employment Taxes.** When you work for an employer, they cover half of your Social Security and Medicare taxes. But when you're self-employed, you're on the hook for both halves—this is called the self-employment tax. As of this book's printing, it's a hefty 15.3%, which includes 12.4% for Social Security and 2.9% for Medicare. This tax is calculated on your net earnings which means after you've subtracted your business expenses, but it's something every small business owner needs to budget for.
- **Estimated Taxes.** Unlike regular employees who have

taxes withheld from their paycheck, small business owners need to pay their taxes quarterly. These estimated tax payments cover both your income taxes and your self-employment taxes. Failing to pay them throughout the year can result in penalties, so it's crucial to stay on top of them.

- **Business Deductions.** One of the perks of owning a business is the ability to deduct business-related expenses. Keep track of every receipt and expense related to your business. This isn't just good bookkeeping—it can also save you a lot come tax time. Business deductions can include: office supplies and equipment, business travel and meals (within certain limits), home office deduction if you work from home, mileage for business travel, and professional services like legal or accounting help.

- **Pass-Through Income**. Many small businesses, like sole proprietorships or LLCs, are treated as pass-through entities. This means the business itself doesn't pay taxes. Instead, the income "passes through" to your personal tax return, where you'll pay taxes at your individual rate. There's also the qualified business income (QBI) deduction, which allows some small business owners to deduct up to 20% of their business income. Check with your accountant to determine whether or not you would quality.

- **Filing Your Taxes as a Business**. As a small business owner, you'll be filing a Schedule C along with your personal tax return which details your business income and expenses. If your business grows, you might consider forming an LLC or S-Corp, which can provide more flexibility and potential tax benefits.

Taxes for small businesses require careful planning. Stay organized, make your estimated payments, and take advantage

MELISSA COX, CFP®

of every deduction available. Consulting a tax professional can help ensure you're filing correctly and not leaving money on the table.

### How to Make Filing Easier: Keep These Documents

One of the best ways to avoid headaches during tax season is to keep track of important documents and receipts throughout the year. Here's what you should hold onto:

- Pay stubs: These help ensure your W-2 is accurate.
- Charitable donation receipts: Keep records of any donations for deductions.
- Medical expenses: If you're deducting medical expenses, save receipts and bills.
- Investment statements: Track any capital gains or losses from investments.
- Business-related expenses: If you're self-employed, save receipts for any business-related costs.

Keeping these documents organized will save you from having to hunt down receipts or from scrambling for information when tax season rolls around. Pro Tip: Consider using a digital organizer or app to scan and store important documents electronically. It's easier to find them later, and you won't have to deal with piles of paper.

### Document Retention: How Long to Keep Your Records

The IRS recommends keeping tax-related documents for at least three years from the date you filed your return in case of an audit or need to amend your filing. However, if you underreported income by more than 25%, you should keep records for six years. If you don't file a return at all (hopefully never the case), you should keep records indefinitely.

As a rule of thumb, here's how long to keep some common documents:

- Tax returns: At least 3-7 years.
- W-2s and 1099s: 3-7 years.
- Investment records: Until you sell the investment, then 3 years after.
- Receipts for deductions: 3 years.

Pro Tip: Keep your tax returns 3-7 years or forever, if possible. It's always helpful to reference previous returns, especially if you move, change jobs, or face a tax audit. But let's operate within some sort of reason—you don't need to keep every single tax document, so don't factor a "file cabinet budget" into your annual expenses. Instead, implement an "I'm stuffed" filing policy or digital copies, and purge.

### Where and How to File Your Taxes

Once you've gathered your documents and completed your tax return, you have a few options for filing:

- Do It Yourself: There's a range of online tax software like TurboTax, H&R Block, or TaxAct that can guide you through the process. If your taxes are fairly simple, this is a cost-effective and easy way to file.
- Hire a Professional: If your taxes are more complicated— maybe you're self-employed, own rental properties, or have significant investments—it might be worth hiring a CPA or tax professional. They'll handle the heavy lifting, and it's nice to have someone in your corner if the IRS has questions.

MELISSA COX, CFP®

- Mail It In: Yes, people still do this! You can print and mail in your return, though it's a bit old-school. The IRS offers e-filing, which is faster and more secure, but if you prefer the snail mail route, go for it. Just make sure to keep a copy of everything you send.

Pro Tip: If you owe taxes, consider scheduling your payment to avoid surprises. Many online systems let you file early and pay closer to the deadline if needed.

### Uncle Sam's Surprises: Estimated Taxes, Audits, and Refunds

Taxes aren't just an annual event for everyone. If you're self-employed or have significant income from investments, you might need to pay estimated taxes throughout the year to avoid a big surprise bill come April. That's right—quarterly payments to our beloved Uncle Sam, just to keep things exciting year-round.

> If you're self-employed or have significant income from investments, you might need to pay estimated taxes throughout the year to avoid a big surprise bill come April.

And then there's the looming threat of an audit. While audits are rare, the idea of the IRS scrutinizing your return can make anyone break out into a cold sweat. Keeping good records and staying on top of your deductions can help you sleep a little better at night.

On the flip side, if you've overpaid, you'll get a tax refund—essentially a repayment of the extra money you gave Uncle Sam. But instead of celebrating that refund as found money, remember it's just a return of your own cash, interest-free. Ideally, you want to aim for a refund that's neither too big nor too small—just right.

## Training Takeaway: Embrace the Inevitable

While taxes may not be the most thrilling part of financial planning, they're unavoidable. Understanding how taxes work, knowing what deductions and credits are available, and staying on top of your payments can make the process a lot less painful—and maybe even a little empowering.

And hey, if you've ever thought about what your final financial gift to Uncle Sam might be, there's an old joke that the last check you write should bounce—hopefully to the IRS.

# Giving Back:
## Charitable Giving and Legacy Planning

Charitable giving might not be at the top of everyone's financial to-do list, but for those who feel called to give back, it's a fantastic way to leave a lasting legacy. Plus, let's face it—nobody wants to give more to the IRS than necessary. If you're going to donate your hard-earned dollars, you might as well do it in a way that benefits both you and the causes close to your heart.

In this chapter, we'll dive into creating a strategic plan for charitable giving that aligns with your values and financial goals—while making sure you keep more of your money out of the IRS's hands. Win-win! (And for any teenagers reading this, let's clarify: A qualified charity does *not* include yourself during times of "desperate need," like concert tickets or a new phone. Sorry, but the IRS won't buy that one.)

### Why Charitable Giving Should Be Part of Your Financial Plan

Some folks are all about philanthropy—it's about supporting a cause, helping the community, or leaving a mark that extends beyond just wealth. And for others, it's more of a side note, which is perfectly okay, too. But if you're in the giving-back camp, it's important to approach it like any other part of your financial plan—strategically.

Charitable giving can come with some sweet tax benefits if you do it right. Let's look at a few strategies to give generously while also reducing that tax bill.

## Qualified Charitable Distribution (QCD)

Tax-free donations made directly from an IRA as distributions to a charity, often counting toward Required Minimum Distributions.

You could donate cash, but if you've got investments that have increased in value, why not give those instead? Donating appreciated assets like stocks lets you skip the capital gains tax *and* claim a tax deduction for the fair market value. More to the charity, less to Uncle Sam—it's like giving your cake and eating it too.

If you're age 70.5 or older and have an IRA, you can make a Qualified Charitable Distribution (QCD). You can donate up to $100,000 per year directly from your IRA to charity. And the best part? It doesn't count as taxable income! At age 73, when you're required to start taking Required Minimum Distributions (RMDs), QCDs can also count toward satisfying your RMD. However, QCDs made prior to age 73 won't apply to future RMDs—only the current year's RMD if you're eligible. It's the perfect tax break for doing good.

You can also establish and give from a Donor-Advised Fund (DAF). Think of a DAF as your personal charitable

MELISSA COX, CFP®

savings account. You get an immediate tax deduction when you contribute, and then you can distribute the money to your favorite charities whenever you're ready. It's like setting your generosity on a slow simmer—perfect for bigger donations during high-income years.

If you're serious about leaving a legacy and want to go big, consider a Charitable Remainder Trust (CRT) or a Charitable Lead Trust (CLT). These trusts let you donate assets, get tax benefits, and either provide income to yourself or your heirs (in the case of a CRT) or give income to charity first (with a CLT). It's a bit more complex but a great way to manage taxes and give back at the same time.

### Leaving a Legacy: It's More Than Just Money

Charitable giving isn't just about writing checks or setting up trusts—it's about passing down your values. Sure, it helps reduce your tax bill, but more importantly, it's a chance to support causes that matter to you and make a real impact. And if done thoughtfully, your charitable giving becomes a way to pass on your principles, not just your dollars.

Your charitable donations should reflect what truly matters to you. Whether it's education, healthcare, the environment, or the arts, your giving plan should align with the values you hold closest. Think of it as a way to put your money where your heart is.

Charitable giving can be a family affair. Involving your kids or grandkids in your charitable planning not only teaches them the importance of giving but also creates a shared family legacy. Whether it's deciding which causes to support or contributing to a family donor-advised fund, making philanthropy a family tradition is one of the most rewarding parts of financial planning.

## The Risks of Giving Too Much (Yes, It's Possible)

It's easy to get caught up in the joy of giving, but over-giving can cause financial stress down the road. While supporting your favorite causes is admirable, it's important to make sure you're still able to meet your own financial needs. After all, you don't want to end up giving away the farm—or your retirement fund!

And remember, giving isn't an all-or-nothing game. If you're still building wealth, you can start small with donations of time, skills, or smaller amounts of money. The key is to make your charitable giving sustainable, ensuring that it works for you now and in the future.

## Training Takeaway: Giving Back While Moving Forward

Charitable giving may not be everyone's top financial goal, but if it's important to you, it's worth doing it right. Creating a strategic giving plan lets you support the causes you care about while making sure you're doing it in the most tax-efficient way possible. Why give more to the government when you can direct those dollars to something you're passionate about? Whether it's donating appreciated assets, setting up a donor-advised fund, or creating a charitable trust, the key is to plan ahead. Make sure your giving aligns with both your financial goals and your values. Done right, your legacy will be more than just a pile of money—it'll be a meaningful contribution to the world.

MELISSA COX, CFP®

# III
# Building

# The Power of Compound Growth

Now that you've started thinking about your financial health and mapped out a plan, it's time to introduce one of my favorite financial concepts: compound growth. If this sounds like something complicated or reserved for math geniuses, don't worry—I'm about to break it down as simply as possible. Because honestly, compound growth is like the magic trick of the financial world. It's one of the most powerful tools out there to help your money grow over time, and once you understand how it works, you'll want to start putting it to use ASAP.

So what exactly is compound growth? In simple terms, it's when your money earns money, and then that new money earns even more money. Think of it like a snowball rolling downhill: The more it grows, the faster it picks up more snow.

Now here's the fun part: Compound growth applies to a variety of investments, not just those with steady returns like CDs, bonds, or mutual funds. It can also apply to stocks. Yes, stocks can be more volatile since their performance depends on the business and market conditions, but over time, many stocks grow in value. When you reinvest dividends (money

MELISSA COX, CFP®

> The magic of compound growth? You don't just earn interest on your original investment; you also earn interest on your interest. And the earlier you start, the more time your money has to grow and multiply.

paid to you by the company for owning their stock), you can benefit from compounding there, too. It's just a little less predictable compared to, say, the interest from a savings account or a bond.

The key takeaway? While the speed of compounding might vary between different types of investments, the principle remains the same: The longer you leave your money invested, the more it can grow on itself. And whether you're investing in CDs, mutual funds, or a diversified portfolio of stocks, compound growth is your best friend when it comes to building long-term wealth.

## Why Thinking Long-Term is The Key to Wealth Accumulation

Let me start with a little scenario. Imagine you've got $100, and you invest it with a return rate of 10% (which, for the sake of this example, we'll assume is pretty solid return for an investment in the stock market). After one year, you've made $10 on that initial $100. Not bad, right? But here's where things get interesting: The next year, you don't just earn another $10. You actually earn $11. Why? Because that 10% return is now working on $110 (your original $100, plus the $10 you already earned).

That, my friends, is compound growth in action. Your money doesn't just earn interest on the original amount—it earns interest on the interest. And the longer you leave it invested, the more powerful that growth becomes. It's like a snowball rolling downhill, picking up more snow and speed as it goes. The earlier you start, the bigger that snowball can grow over time.

While compound growth might not look all that impressive in the first few years, over the long haul, it becomes a game-changer. The longer you give it, the more that snowball keeps rolling, building wealth in ways that seem almost effortless.

### The Magic of Compound Interest and Early Investments

Here's a fun fact: Albert Einstein is rumored to have called compound interest "the eighth wonder of the world." Now I can't confirm if Einstein actually said that (he was a busy guy, after all), but the sentiment is spot-on. Compound interest is the gift that keeps on giving, especially if you start early.

Let's say you start investing at 25 years old and contribute $200 a month to a retirement account with an average annual return of 8%. By the time you're 65, you'll have contributed $96,000 of your own money—but thanks to compound growth, your account will have grown to over $700,000. Not too shabby, right?

Now, let's compare that to someone who starts investing

> **Dollar-Cost Averaging (DCA)**
>
> An investment strategy whereby an investor invests a fixed amount of money into a particular asset, regardless of its price, or market conditions. By spreading purchases over time, the investor creates an average cost per share.

at 35 instead of 25. They invest the same $200 a month with the same return rate, but because they started 10 years later, their account will have grown to about $300,000 by age 65. That's a big difference for starting just a decade later! The lesson? *Time is your greatest ally when it comes to building wealth. The earlier you start, the more time your money has to grow and multiply.*

So if you're in your 20s or 30s and feeling like you're too young to think about retirement, trust me—your future self will be *so grateful* if you start now. And if you're in your 40s or 50s and just getting started, don't worry—it's never too late to take advantage of compound growth. It just means you might need to contribute a little more to make up for lost time. But don't let that discourage you. Even starting later can have a huge impact.

### The Power of Dollar-Cost Averaging (DCA)

Let's talk about one of the simplest yet most effective strategies for taking advantage of compound growth: Dollar-Cost Averaging (DCA). This means investing a fixed amount of money at regular intervals, regardless of what the market is doing.

For example, you might invest $500 every month, whether the market is up, down, or sideways. By doing this, you buy more shares when prices are low and fewer shares when prices are high, which can lower the overall cost of your investments over time.

DCA is great because it takes the emotion out of investing. No more guessing about whether it's the right time to jump in or out of the market. You're consistently investing, and over the long term, this strategy helps smooth out the bumps of market volatility.

### Staying Invested: Lessons from Market Crashes

One of the most common mistakes investors make is pulling their money out of the market when things start to look bleak. When the market starts declining, fear kicks in, and people hit the panic button. The problem? They often pull out at the worst possible time and miss out on the best days in the market which frequently follow the worst days.

Here's the harsh truth: When you pull your money out in fear, you lock in those losses. Even worse, by the time the market starts to recover, many investors are still sitting on the sidelines trying to "time" their way back in. This leads to another missed opportunity—getting back in after the market has already bounced back. They wait for signs of stability, and by the time they feel confident again, they've already missed significant gains.

A study from Fidelity showed that over a 30-year period an investor who missed just the five best-performing days in the market would have seen significantly lower returns compared to someone who stayed fully invested the whole time.

MELISSA COX, CFP®

> Market crashes are inevitable, but so is the recovery. The real challenge lies not in avoiding crashes but in staying invested *through* them.

It's a powerful reminder: The market's biggest rebounds often follow its steepest declines, and getting scared out of the game means missing out on the recovery.

## The Psychological Trap of Market Timing

Market crashes trigger the fight-or-flight response that's hardwired into us. It's natural to want to pull out, regroup, and wait for better days. But here's where the behavioral finance trap kicks in: We're often terrible at predicting when those better days will come. Trying to time the market feels like regaining control, but it often backfires.

Many investors who pull their money out during a crash find themselves stuck in "decision paralysis" afterward. They don't want to jump back in too soon, fearing another downturn, and by the time they feel comfortable again, the market is back at or near its peak. The opportunities for growth? Missed.

Here's where understanding behavioral finance can really save your future wealth. Instead of giving in to panic, staying invested through downturns allows you to take advantage of the eventual market recovery. Yes, it's tough to watch the value of your portfolio fall, but over the long term, history shows that markets recover, and investors who stay the course typically come out ahead. This ties back to the principle of compound growth—money left in the market continues to grow even through volatility. The key is to resist emotional reactions and stick to your long-term strategy.

Market crashes are inevitable, but so is the recovery. The real challenge lies not in avoiding crashes but in staying invested through them. By understanding and managing your emotions, you can avoid the trap of market timing and set yourself up for long-term success.

### Shifting Your Mindset from Quick Wins to Sustainable Growth

In today's world, we're all about instant gratification, right? I get it. We love quick wins—the thrill of snagging a bargain, making a fast buck, or watching a stock jump overnight. But here's the deal: True financial success isn't about winning the lottery or hitting it big with the next hot stock tip. It's about slow, steady, *sustainable* growth over time. That's where the magic happens.

It's easy to get caught up in the excitement of trying to make quick gains (especially when the latest financial "guru" on social media promises you can double your money in a month). But those quick wins often come with high risks. Compound growth, on the other hand, is like the tortoise in the story of the tortoise and the hare. It may not be flashy or exciting at first, but it's steady, reliable, and most importantly, it works. I've had clients come to me who were obsessed with finding the "next big thing" in investing. They'd jump from stock to stock, chasing trends, and they would sometimes make a little money. But more often than not, they'd end up frustrated when the market didn't go their way.

MELISSA COX, CFP®

This reminds me of what Peter Lynch said in his book *One Up On Wall Street*, the first book I read when I started my career as a financial planner. He was the legendary investor who created one of Fidelity's largest mutual funds, the Fidelity Magellan Fund. Lynch said, "As an average investor, by the time you heard about the latest and greatest money-making stock, it's likely on the way back down because people have made money on it." And that's just as true today as it was back then, especially with the speed at which information spreads electronically.

I've seen it firsthand. Clients hear about the next "hot stock" from the news or a friend, only to jump in right as the stock began its descent. Eventually, these same clients would sit down and say, "Okay, let's just focus on a long-term plan." And you know what? Those are the clients who end up building the most wealth over time. Because, as Lynch and many years of experience have taught me, slow and steady wins the race.

### How Compound Growth Fits Into Your Financial Plan

Now that we've established that compound growth is your new best friend, how do you incorporate it into your financial plan? It all comes down to two key factors: time and consistency.

I know you've already heard me say this, but I really can't stress it enough: The earlier you start investing, the more time your money has to grow. Even if you can only contribute a small amount each month, start now. Over time, that small amount will grow into something much bigger. And be consistent by contributing regularly to your investments. This could mean setting up automatic transfers to your retirement account or regularly investing a percentage of your income. The key is to make it a habit, so you don't have to think about it. Just set it and forget it—and let compound growth do its thing.

Markets go up and down. That's just how it works. But if you stay invested through the ups and downs, your money will continue to grow over time. Compound growth thrives on consistency and patience, so resist the urge to sell off your investments during a market dip.

If you're receiving dividends or interest on your investments, reinvest them. This is how compound growth works— your returns are added to your original investment, and then *both* start earning more returns. It's a snowball effect, and reinvesting is how you keep that snowball rolling.

### Training Takeaway:
### Harnessing the Power of Time and Consistency

The most important takeaway here is that time is on your side. Compound growth is a slow and steady process, but the results can be life-changing if you give it enough time to work its magic. Whether you're 25 or 55, it is important to get started—and stay consistent.

So while you're busy living your life, building your career, and enjoying the present, thanks to the power of compound growth, know that your money is working behind the scenes to secure your future. Now that's something worth celebrating.

And remember, this is all part of *your race, your pace.* There's no need to rush or compete with anyone else. The best financial decisions are the ones that fit your timeline and your goals. Compound growth is here for the long haul—just like you.

MELISSA COX, CFP®

# The Importance of Investing (And Why The Right Accounts Matter More Than You Think)

Before we dive into the fascinating world of stocks, bonds, and the occasional roller-coaster ride that is the investment market, there's something we need to address: *Where* you're putting your money might actually be just as important as *what* you're investing in.

When it comes to long-term financial success, especially when planning for retirement, the types of accounts you use can make all the difference. It's not just about picking great investments—it's about making sure those investments are working for you in the most tax-efficient way possible.

If you're not paying attention to how different types of investment accounts work, Uncle Sam might end up taking more of your hard-earned returns than necessary. That's where the concept of tax-deferred vs. taxable investments comes into play—and why understanding the hierarchy between different types of accounts is key to a solid investment strategy.

### Understanding the Different Types of Investment Accounts

When people think about investing, they usually jump straight to what they want to buy—stocks, mutual funds, real estate, or whatever new hot thing their neighbor's been talking about. But equally important is *where* those investments are held. Broadly speaking, investment accounts fall into two main categories: tax-deferred and taxable. Understanding the differences between these types of accounts will help you build a strategy that not only grows your money but also keeps more of it in your pocket come tax time.

**401(k), 403(b), IRA, Roth IRA, SIMPLE IRA, SEP IRA**

A variety of accounts—each wiith its own requirements—that provide tax benefits to help you save for retirement.

Tax-deferred accounts are your retirement accounts—the golden ticket when it comes to long-term investing for the future. Tax-deferred accounts allow you to contribute money before taxes are taken out (or sometimes after, in the case of Roth accounts), and the investments within these accounts grow tax-free until you withdraw the funds. Examples of tax-deferred accounts include:

- 401(k) and 403(b): Employer-sponsored retirement plans that allow you to contribute pre-tax dollars (or after-tax with a Roth 401(k)). Many employers even offer matching contributions, which is basically free money.
- Traditional IRA: An individual retirement account where you can contribute pre-tax dollars and allow your investments to grow tax-deferred until you begin withdrawals in retirement.
- Roth IRA: With a Roth IRA, you contribute after-tax dollars, but the major benefit is that your withdrawals in

MELISSA COX, CFP®

> Tax efficiency is a crucial part of a successful investment strategy. By focusing on the right accounts first, you're allowing your investments to grow in a tax-advantaged environment. More of your money stays invested and grows over time.

retirement (including all the growth) are tax-free.

- SEP IRA and SIMPLE IRA: If you're self-employed or own a small business, a SEP IRA (Simplified Employee Pension) or SIMPLE IRA (Savings Incentive Match Plan for Employees) allows you to make significant pre-tax contributions to a retirement account. These accounts are ideal for small business owners and freelancers who want to save for retirement while reducing taxable income.

Here's why tax-deferred accounts are so powerful: When you don't have to pay taxes on your investment growth year after year, that money can keep compounding without Uncle Sam taking a cut along the way. The longer you leave those investments to grow, the more potential you have for serious wealth accumulation by the time you retire.

Unlike tax-deferred accounts, taxable investment accounts don't give you any tax breaks upfront or down the line. Every year, you'll be taxed on any dividends, interest, or capital gains your investments generate, even if you don't withdraw the money. While that might sound like a bummer compared to the tax benefits of a retirement account, taxable accounts have their own advantages.

Taxable accounts include brokerage accounts (for buying and selling stocks, bonds, mutual funds, etc.) and high-yield savings accounts, which allow you to earn interest at higher rates than standard savings accounts, though they're still subject to income tax. For those interested in the flexibility of investing without retirement account restrictions, taxable accounts are a useful addition to your financial strategy.

The upside of taxable accounts is flexibility. You're not limited by contribution limits, like you are with retirement accounts, and you can access the funds whenever you need them, though you'll need to be mindful of capital gains taxes. Taxable accounts also give you the freedom to invest in ways that may not be available within a retirement account—like in real estate or in certain types of individual stocks.

### The Hierarchy of Investments: Where to Invest First

So now that we know the difference between tax-deferred and taxable accounts, let's talk about the *hierarchy* of investing. When building your investment strategy, it's important to prioritize where you're putting your money based on the tax advantages of different accounts. This can maximize your growth and minimize what you owe in taxes later on. Here's the hierarchy I suggest, and why:

1. Start with Employer-Matched 401(k) Contributions. If your employer offers a 401(k) or 403(b) with a matching contribution, this is where you should focus first.

Employer matches are essentially free money—it's like getting an immediate 100% return on your investment, and who wouldn't want that? Contribute at least enough to get the full match, because leaving that money on the table is like walking away from a raise.

2. Max Out Your Roth IRA (If You're Eligible). Next, if you're eligible, contribute to a Roth IRA. The beauty of the Roth IRA is in its future tax benefits: Your contributions grow tax-free, and withdrawals in retirement are also tax-free. This is especially valuable if you expect to be in a higher tax bracket later in life. The Roth IRA also gives you more investment choices and flexibility compared to a traditional 401(k) or 403(b). The downside? There are income limits to qualify for contributing to a Roth IRA, and annual contribution limits are relatively low (currently $6,500 per year for those under age 50, and $7,500 for those 50 or older). But if you can, take advantage of this account's tax-free growth and future tax savings.

3. Contribute to Tax-Deferred Accounts (401(k), Traditional IRA). After maxing out your Roth IRA, the next step is to contribute more to your employer-sponsored retirement plan (such as a 401(k) or 403(b)) or a traditional IRA. These accounts allow for tax-deferred growth, which means your investments compound faster because you're not paying taxes on gains until you withdraw the money in retirement. If you've already contributed enough to get your employer match and still have more to save, focus on maxing out these accounts before moving to taxable investments. The tax-deferral means more money is working for you in the long run.

4. Invest in Taxable Accounts. Once you've maxed out your tax-deferred options, it's time to consider investing in taxable accounts. These accounts provide flexibility—you can access your money anytime, unlike retirement accounts that impose penalties for early withdrawals. Just keep in mind that the growth in these accounts is subject to capital gains tax, so it's important to be strategic about what you invest in here.

## Why Tax Efficiency Matters More Than You Think

Tax efficiency is a crucial part of a successful investment strategy. By focusing on the right accounts first (like your 401(k), Roth IRA, or traditional IRA), you're allowing your investments to grow in a tax-advantaged environment, meaning more of your money stays invested and grows over time.

Many people focus so much on the returns they can get from different investments that they overlook the role taxes play in chipping away at their wealth. Being strategic about which accounts you use can boost your long-term financial success without having to take on extra risk in the stock market.

## Training Takeaway: Building a Strong Investment Foundation

Before you even start picking investments, building the right foundation for your portfolio starts with understanding which accounts to prioritize. Taking advantage of tax-advantaged accounts like 401(k)s, IRAs, and Roth IRAs allows your money to work harder for you by minimizing the tax burden. Once you've

MELISSA COX, CFP®

made the most of those opportunities, you can use taxable accounts to continue growing your wealth with greater flexibility.

Investing is one of the most important tools for building long-term wealth, and knowing where to place your money is half the battle. With the right account strategy in place, you can let your investments grow without worrying about giving up too much to taxes. And as we'll see in the next chapter, once you've got the account structure in place, choosing the right investments can put you on the path to financial freedom.

# 21

## Understanding the World of Investments

Investing can sometimes feel like learning a new language—one filled with terms, ideas, and charts that can seem intimidating at first glance. But investing doesn't have to be complicated. Once you understand the basic types of investments and how they work, you'll be in a much better position to make informed decisions that support your financial goals.

This chapter is designed to give you a broad understanding of the most common types of investments, how they function, and why people choose them. Whether you're just getting started or looking to fine-tune your investment strategy, this overview will help you navigate the investment landscape with more confidence. And always remember: No matter how simple or exciting an investment may seem, it's crucial to do your homework, understand the risks involved, and be aware of any fees before jumping in.

### The Basics: Why Do People Invest?

At its core, investing is about putting your money to work for you. Rather than keeping all your savings in cash that

MELISSA COX, CFP®

> Every investment carries some level of risk. There is always the possibility that you could lose money. But the right strategies and knowledge can help you reach your goals while managing those risks.

generally loses value over time due to inflation, investing allows you to grow your wealth over time. The idea is that by putting your money into different types of assets that can increase in value and earn you returns—like stocks, bonds, or real estate—investing can help you achieve long-term financial goals like retirement, buying a home, or even building generational wealth.

Of course, the flip side of investing is *risk*. Every investment carries some level of risk, meaning there's always the possibility that you could lose money. But with the right strategies and knowledge, you can build a diversified portfolio that balances risk with potential rewards, helping you reach your goals while managing those risks.

Let's break down the most common types of investments and discuss why people use them.

### Stocks

When you buy a stock, you're buying a small piece of ownership in a company. Think of it like buying a slice of a pizza—you own part of the whole pie. If the company does well, the value of your stock may go up, allowing you to sell it for more than you paid. In some cases, companies may also pay dividends, which are a portion of the company's profits distributed to shareholders.

Stocks offer the potential for higher returns compared to other types of investments. In fact, over the long term, the stock market has historically provided strong returns, helping investors grow their wealth. But stocks are volatile, meaning their value can fluctuate significantly in the short term. If the company you've invested in performs poorly, your stock could lose value or even become worthless.

Before investing in any stock, research the company's financial health, leadership, and long-term growth potential. Stocks can be risky, so it's important to diversify by holding shares in multiple companies or invest in mutual funds or exchange-traded funds (ETFs).

## Bonds

When you buy a bond, you're essentially lending money to a government or corporation. In return, they agree to pay you interest over a set period and return your original investment (called the "principal") when the bond matures.

Bonds are generally considered safer than stocks as they provide steady, predictable income in the form of interest payments. They can act as a stabilizer in your portfolio, reducing overall risk, especially during market downturns.

Bonds carry interest-rate risk. If interest rates rise, the value of existing bonds tends to fall because new bonds will offer higher interest rates. If the issuer (government or corporation) defaults, you could lose some or all of your investment.

MELISSA COX, CFP®

While bonds are generally safer than stocks, they come with lower returns. They're a good option for those looking for stability and a predictable income stream, especially as you approach retirement.

### Mutual Funds: A Pool of Investments

A mutual fund pools money from many investors to buy a diversified portfolio of stocks, bonds, or other securities. When you buy shares of a mutual fund, you're buying a small piece of all the investments the fund holds.

Consequently, mutual funds offer instant diversification, reducing risk by spreading your money across many different investments. They're managed by professional fund managers, saving you time and effort compared to picking individual stocks and bonds yourself.

Mutual funds do come with management fees which can eat into your returns over time. And while diversification helps reduce risk, mutual funds can still lose value, especially if the markets perform poorly.

Make sure to understand the fees associated with the mutual fund (expense ratios) and what types of investments it holds. Different funds have different risk levels, so choose one that aligns with your goals and risk tolerance.

### Exchange-Traded Funds (ETFs)

ETFs are similar to mutual funds in that they offer diversification by holding a basket of different investments. However, ETFs are traded on stock exchanges—meaning you can buy and sell them throughout the trading day, just like individual stocks. ETFs offer low-cost diversification, often with lower fees than mutual funds. And they do provide flexibility, allowing you to buy or sell shares throughout the day as market prices change.

Like mutual funds, however, ETFs are subject to market risk. If the underlying assets perform poorly, the value of the ETF can fall. Some ETFs track niche markets or sectors which can be riskier than more diversified options.

ETFs are a great option for cost-conscious investors looking for diversification. Be sure to check the ETF's expense ratio and what assets it holds to ensure it aligns with your values and investment strategy.

### Real Estate: Physical Property as an Investment

Investing in real estate involves purchasing physical property—residential homes, commercial buildings, or rental properties—with the goal of earning income or appreciation over time. Real estate can provide both income (through rental payments) and long-term growth (through property appreciation). It's a tangible asset, meaning you own something physical that holds value.

But investing in real estate requires significant upfront capital and ongoing expenses, such as maintenance, taxes, and property management. And real estate markets can be unpredictable, and property values can decrease, especially in economic downturns.

**Real Estate Investment Trust (REIT)**

Companies that own or finance income-producing real estate, allowing investors to earn returns without owning property directly.

Real estate can be a good diversification tool, but it's important to consider the time, effort, and costs involved in managing property.

You can also invest in real estate through Real Estate Investment Trusts (REITs), which allow you to invest in real estate without owning physical property.

## Commodities

Commodities include raw materials like gold, oil, and agricultural products. Investors can buy commodities directly or invest in commodity-related funds or futures contracts. Commodities can serve as a hedge against inflation as their prices often rise when inflation increases. They can diversify your portfolio by adding an asset class that doesn't always move in sync with stocks and bonds.

The bad news is that commodity prices can be volatile and influenced by factors outside of your control—such as weather, geopolitical events, and supply-demand dynamics. Consequently, investing directly in commodities or futures can be complex and risky for beginners. Instead, you could consider commodity-focused ETFs or mutual funds as a way to gain exposure without the complexity of direct commodity investing.

Commodities are something I get asked about a lot—especially when it comes to gold and silver. They are one of the more colorful and unpredictable asset types. People often want to know whether they should be investing in precious metals or other raw materials, like oil or agricultural products. Unlike stocks or bonds, where you're investing in companies or debt, commodities represent the basic goods that the global economy depends on. While they can offer protection against inflation, investing in commodities also comes with its own unique risks and rewards, which makes understanding them crucial before diving in.

Commodities are often used as a hedge against inflation, making them valuable in times of rising prices. When the cost of goods increases, commodities like oil or grain tend to go up in value, helping balance out your portfolio.

However, investing in commodities can come with unique risks—and sometimes, some pretty amusing (or disastrous) stories.

They are generally more volatile than other types of investments and often traded through futures contracts which can amplify both potential gains and risks.

Thankfully, there are now funds and ETFs that specialize in commodities, making it easier for investors to gain exposure without directly buying and selling raw materials themselves. Whether you're considering investments in gold, oil, agriculture, or something more niche (like pork bellies), these funds allow for a more diversified and manageable approach. Still, it's critical to understand how a futures contract works and to assess your risk tolerance before diving in.

### A Cautionary Tale: The Pork Belly Near Miss

When I first started in the financial industry, I heard a story about someone who decided to "play" with commodities, specifically pork bellies, which are used to make bacon. This person got a little too deep into futures contracts without fully understanding how they work.

A futures contract is an agreement to buy or sell a specific amount of a commodity at a set price on a specific future date.

MELISSA COX, CFP®

> **Futures Contract**
>
> A legal agreement to buy or sell a specific asset at a predetermined price on a set future date. Commonly used for hedging or speculative purposes, it obligates both parties to fulfill the terms of the contract, regardless of market conditions at the time of settlement.

If you don't close out the contract—which means selling it to someone else or canceling it— before it matures, you might actually have to take delivery of the commodity.

In this case, the investor narrowly dodged having a truckload of pork bellies delivered straight to their driveway! Can you imagine waking up to find a shipment of raw pork sitting in front of your house?

It's a funny story now, but it's also a great example of why it's important to understand exactly what you're getting into when you invest in commodities. Not everyone is equipped to store thousands of pounds of bacon.

### The Power of Smart Commodities Investing: Herb Kelleher and Jet-Fuel Futures

On the flip side, commodities can be a brilliant investment when done thoughtfully and strategically. A great example of this is how Herb Kelleher, the legendary founder of Southwest Airlines, saved the company millions by investing in jet-fuel futures during the 1980s and 1990s.

At a time when fuel prices were highly volatile, Kelleher bet that locking in future fuel prices through futures contracts would shield Southwest from rising costs. By taking action, Southwest managed to secure lower fuel prices for years, saving the airline a fortune and giving it a major competitive edge. While other airlines were struggling with skyrocketing fuel costs, Southwest remained profitable, thanks to this savvy commodities investment.

Kelleher's strategy with jet-fuel futures is a reminder that commodities, when used wisely, can play a significant role in managing risk and protecting against market volatility.

### Do Your Homework: Understanding Risks and Fees

No matter which type of investment you choose, it's important to fully understand what you're getting into. Every investment comes with its own set of risks and fees, and failing to understand them can lead to unpleasant surprises down the road.

Before investing, you need to research the investment's performance history and future outlook. While past performance doesn't guarantee future results, it can give you a sense of how an investment might behave in different market conditions.

Remember that fees—whether the management fees of a mutual fund or the transaction fees associated with trading stocks—can eat into your returns over time. Make sure you know what you're paying for.

And pay close attention to the risks you're taking. Some investments are riskier than others. Be honest with yourself about how much risk you're comfortable with, and choose investments that align with your financial goals and risk tolerance.

MELISSA COX, CFP®

*Training Takeaway:*
*Building a Balanced Investment Portfolio*

Investing isn't about picking the "perfect" investment—it's about building a balanced portfolio that matches your financial goals, risk tolerance, and timeline. Diversifying your investments across different asset classes—like stocks, bonds, and real estate—can help reduce risk while giving your portfolio room to grow. Above all, do your homework before you invest. Understanding the risks and fees associated with each type of investment will help you avoid surprises and put you on the path to financial success.

Remember that working with a financial planner can take most of that burden off your shoulders. Financial planners do the research and vetting for you, so you don't have to dig into every single company or investment option. They're there to guide you with expert insights, keeping your goals in focus and ensuring that your investments are aligned with your long-term strategy.

# Diversification and Inflation-Proofing Your Future

In the previous chapter, we discussed the different types of assets you can invest in—stocks, bonds, real estate, and more. Now, it's time to build on that foundation and introduce one of the true superheroes of financial planning: diversification. But every superhero has a nemesis, and in this case, it's none other than the slow-drip villain of your portfolio: inflation.

Diversification and inflation protection are the ultimate tag team when it comes to managing your investments. Together, they help you reduce risk and maintain your purchasing power over time, making sure your hard-earned money doesn't lose value while you're on the road to financial freedom. In this chapter, we'll explore how these two forces can either work for—or against—you, and how to build a portfolio that stands strong in the face of both market volatility and rising prices.

Diversification is a fancy term for spreading your money across different types of investments to reduce risk. Instead of putting all your money in one stock, bond, or sector, diversification means holding a variety of assets. This way, if one investment performs poorly, the others can help cushion

> Diversification is like having a permanent back-up plan: If one part of your portfolio struggles, the rest of your investments can help keep you on track. The idea is to create a portfolio that balances risk and reward in a way that aligns with your financial goals.

the blow. It's like having a backup plan: If one part of your portfolio struggles, the rest of your investments can help keep you on track.

Diversification means investing in a mix of asset types (stocks, bonds, real estate, etc.), spreading your investments across different sectors (technology, healthcare, energy, etc.). It also means holding assets of companies, of a variety of sizes—also known as their capitalization or market cap (large-cap, mid-cap, small-cap, micro-cap, and mega-cap companies). Because each asset type behaves differently in specific market conditions, diversification helps spread out your risk.

The idea is to create a portfolio that balances risk and reward in a way that aligns with your financial goals. It's perfectly okay to take some risks, especially if you're early in your investing journey and have time to recover from market downturns. But diversification ensures that those risks are spread out, so one bad investment doesn't derail your entire plan.

## Diversifying by Asset Types

Diversifying your stock holdings across different industries and regions can reduce risk. For example, if technology stocks are having a rough year, your holdings in healthcare or energy might still perform well. Stocks are your go-to asset for long-term growth, but they can be volatile in the short term, which is why it's important to balance them with other asset types.

Bonds are generally more stable than stocks, offering fixed income over time. However, they don't provide the same high returns as stocks. By including bonds in your portfolio, you balance the volatility of stocks with the safety of more stable assets. You can also diversify within bonds by holding government, corporate, and municipal bonds, each with different risk profiles.

Investing in real estate—either through physical properties or Real Estate Investment Trusts—can add another layer of diversification. Real estate often behaves differently than stocks and bonds, providing income through rent or dividends while also appreciating in value over time.

Commodities, private equity, or hedge funds tend to be more specialized and carry higher risks, so they should be used sparingly and strategically. They're like the wild cards in your portfolio—a little goes a long way.

## Diversifying by Size: Market Capitalization

Another key aspect of diversification is holding investments of different sizes, or market capitalizations. When we talk about "market cap," we're referring to the total value of a company's outstanding shares. It's like ranking companies by

MELISSA COX, CFP®

their size, from the scrappy startups to the corporate giants. And yes, investing size does matter—but not always in the way you think. Bigger isn't always better, and smaller can offer some exciting growth opportunities.

Diversifying across different market caps allows you to balance growth potential with stability. Smaller companies tend to grow faster but are more volatile—like the energetic kid on a sugar high—while larger companies are more stable like that dependable friend who shows up with coffee and a plan. The key is finding the right mix of both to keep your portfolio steady without missing out on potential big gains.

Mega-cap stocks are the absolute giants—the global titans that dominate their industries. Companies like Apple, Microsoft, and Amazon fall into this category, with market values exceeding $200 billion. Mega-cap stocks offer stability and are generally less volatile because they have established revenue streams and global reach. They may not deliver the fastest growth, but they provide consistent returns and are often considered the safe bets in a portfolio.

Just a notch down from mega-caps, large-cap stocks have market values between $10 billion and $200 billion. Think of companies like Coca-Cola, VISA, or Procter & Gamble. These firms are established, stable, and often have global operations. While they might not experience the wild growth swings of smaller companies, they offer solid returns and lower risk, making them a core part of a diversified portfolio.

Mid-cap companies have market values between $2 billion and $10 billion. These companies—such as Domino's Pizza, The New York Times, and Under Armour—are often in a high-growth phase, but they've also proven they have staying power. They tend to offer a nice balance between growth and stability—riskier than large caps but less volatile than small caps. Think of mid-cap stocks as the up-and-comers that are on their way to becoming large-cap firms.

Small-cap stocks have market values between $300 million and $2 billion, and they're where you'll find a lot of growth potential—but also more risk. Small-cap stocks are often younger companies that haven't yet established themselves as industry leaders. They can provide huge returns if they succeed, but they can also be more volatile and subject to market swings. Think of companies that are just emerging in new markets or developing cutting-edge technologies such as Cracker Barrel, Crocs, and YETI.

Micro-cap stocks are the Wild West of investing, with market values between $50 million and $300 million. These are small, speculative companies, often new or in niche industries. Micro-caps—including Timberland and Sirius XM Holdings—can offer massive upside potential, but they come with extreme risk. It's not uncommon for these companies to have limited liquidity and to be subject to wild price swings, which means you can make or lose a lot of money very quickly. These are high-risk, high-reward investments that should be approached with caution.

### The Silent Wealth "Eroder"—Inflation

Before we jump into why diversification is so important for fighting inflation, let's take a moment to spotlight the villain of this story: Inflation is like the slow leak in your finances that you don't notice until your tires are flat. It quietly chips away at the value of your money over time, and before you know it, your carefully saved dollars don't stretch as far

MELISSA COX, CFP®

> Just like you make sure your house is built to weather storms, you need to make sure your financial plan can withstand the constant drizzle of inflation. Inflation-proofing your wealth isn't just a good idea; it's essential.

as they used to. When building your financial future, you can't ignore the impact inflation has on your wealth. Just like you'd make sure your house is built to weather storms, you need to make sure your financial plan can withstand the constant drizzle of inflation.

Imagine that you've saved up $1 million for retirement (not too shabby). If inflation averages 3% a year, in 20 years, that $1 million might feel more like $550,000. That's why inflation-proofing your wealth isn't just a good idea; it's essential.

The key to successfully combining diversification with inflation protection is balance. You want to hold a balanced mix of stocks, bonds, real estate, and commodities because each plays a role in responding to inflation differently.

You might want to consider Treasury Inflation-Protected Securities (TIPS) and other inflation-protected assets to ensure that a portion of your portfolio directly adjusts for rising prices. TIPS are bonds issued by the U.S. Treasury that are designed to protect your investment from inflation. The principal value of TIPS increases with inflation and decreases with deflation, as measured by the Consumer Price Index (CPI). This makes them an excellent tool for safeguarding your purchasing power over time.

You can also look for investments that provide a reliable income stream, like dividend-paying stocks or rental properties. Income-producing assets can help you stay ahead of in-

> **Treasury Inflation-Protected Securities (TIPS)**
>
> U.S. Treasury bonds indexed to inflation, protecting investors from the decline in purchasing power over time.

flation by providing regular cash flow that increases over time.

One of the biggest threats inflation poses in retirement is its impact on healthcare costs. Healthcare expenses tend to rise faster than general inflation, and these costs can quickly eat into your retirement savings if you're not prepared.

Make sure you understand the costs associated with Medicare, and consider supplemental insurance to cover what Medicare doesn't. Just because Medicare kicks in at 65 doesn't mean your healthcare costs disappear—it's crucial to budget for premiums, out-of-pocket expenses, and any additional services you may need.

Health Savings Accounts (HSAs) are a great tool for combating healthcare inflation. Contributions are tax-deductible, and withdrawals for qualified medical expenses are tax-free. Plus, the funds can be invested and grow tax-free over time, helping you build a buffer against rising medical costs. However, not everyone is eligible for an HSA. You must be enrolled in a high-deductible health plan (HDHP) to open one. This applies to both W-2 employees and self-employed individuals as long as their health plan qualifies as an HDHP.

MELISSA COX, CFP®

Before we completely villainize inflation, it's important to recognize that inflation isn't always the enemy. While *runaway* inflation can wreak havoc, *moderate* inflation is a sign of a growing economy, and it can actually benefit certain investments.

A "normal" inflation rate tends to fall between 2% and 3% per year. At this level, inflation reflects a healthy economy with rising wages and increasing demand for goods and services. But inflation can also get out of control, as seen in the 1980s, when the United States experienced double-digit inflation. More recently in the 2020s, when inflation spiked dramatically due to a combination of factors—including supply chain disruptions, increased consumer demand, rising energy costs, and the economic ripple effects of COVID-19—we also saw damaging inflation. The pandemic's impact on global production and distribution played a significant role in pushing inflation higher than usual, reminding us how quickly economic conditions can shift.

However, moderate inflation can offer some benefits. Inflation often accompanies wage growth, meaning that as prices rise, people (ideally) earn more money. This allows you to keep pace with the cost of living. So if your income is rising faster than inflation, you're staying ahead of the game.

Inflation can be good for homeowners and real estate investors. As prices go up, the value of real estate tends to increase as well, creating appreciation for property owners. Rents also rise with inflation, so owning rental properties can become even more lucrative.

For borrowers, inflation can actually be helpful. If you have a fixed-rate mortgage or other fixed-rate debt, inflation erodes the value of that debt over time. In other words, you're paying back your loan with dollars that are worth less than when you originally borrowed them.

Certain stocks, particularly those in industries like energy or consumer goods, tend to perform well during inflationary periods because companies can raise prices in line with inflation. Commodities like gold or oil also tend to rise in value with inflation which makes them solid inflation hedges.

So you see, inflation isn't all bad when you understand it—it's part of the natural economic cycle. The key is understanding how it works and positioning your investments to benefit from it when possible.

### The Risks of Not Diversifying

So what happens if you don't diversify? The short answer: You're walking a tightrope without a safety net. If your portfolio is too concentrated in one area—whether that's a single stock, one sector, or even one asset class—you're exposing yourself to a much higher risk than you should.

For example, imagine having all your money invested in one company, and that company suddenly goes bankrupt. You've just lost everything. Even large, well-established companies can stumble, so spreading your investments across different stocks and sectors protects you from losing your entire portfolio to one bad bet.

What if you've heavily invested in one sector, say technology, and there's a major downturn in that industry? If all your investments are tied to that one sector, your portfolio takes a hit, and you could lose a significant portion of your wealth.

Investing solely in one country or region can also be risky.

Economic or political instability, regulatory changes, or even natural disasters can impact an entire country's market. By diversifying globally, you spread your risk across many economies.

Without diversification, you might miss out on sectors or markets that are booming while your investments lag behind. A well-diversified portfolio ensures you're capturing growth opportunities across a range of assets, sectors, and regions, while also protecting against downturns in any one area.

In short, not diversifying is like playing the lottery with your financial future. Sure, you might hit the jackpot, but it's more likely that you'll end up with a losing ticket. Diversification helps smooth out the bumps in the road and increases your chances of long-term success.

### Have Fun, But Stay Smart

One of the great things about having a diversified portfolio is that it gives you the flexibility to have a little fun with your investments without taking on too much risk. If you're someone who enjoys the thrill of picking individual stocks or investing in the latest hot trend (hello, cryptocurrency!), diversification allows you to do that in a way that won't put your entire financial future in jeopardy.

Think of your portfolio as having a "core" and "satellite" approach. Your core investments should be diversified across asset types, sectors, and market caps. These are the steady, long-term investments that will carry you through to your financial goals. The satellite portion of your portfolio can be where you take a few calculated risks—picking individual stocks, experimenting with new sectors, or investing in niche markets.

The key is to limit the amount of money you allocate to

these high-risk investments. By keeping them a small per-centage of your overall portfolio, you can enjoy the excitement of active investing without risking your financial security.

### Training Takeaway: The Art of Balanced Risk and Inflation Protection

Diversification and inflation-proofing aren't just two sepa-rate strategies—they're two sides of the same coin. When you diversify your portfolio, you're not only reducing risk but also laying the groundwork for inflation protection by including assets that tend to perform well when prices rise.

A well-diversified portfolio balances higher-risk, high-er-reward investments (like small-cap stocks or emerging markets) with more stable, lower-risk assets (like bonds or large-cap stocks). The idea is to have different pieces of your portfolio working together to reduce overall volatility while still giving you opportunities for growth.

Diversification isn't about avoiding risk entirely, because let's face it, all investing involves risk. It's about *managing* risk, making informed decisions, and giving your portfolio the best possible chance of weathering whatever the market throws at you. Inflation protection comes naturally as part of that bal-ance. With the right balance of diversification and inflation protection, you're setting yourself up for long-term success. You're not just playing the game—you're also giving yourself the best shot to win, even when the market takes a few unex-pected turns.

So go ahead, take some calculated risks, have a little fun with your satellite portfolio, and make sure you're always keep-ing an eye on the bigger picture. With the right strategy, you

MELISSA COX, CFP®

can navigate both market volatility and inflationary pressures, keeping your financial future on track.

## Building Retirement Wealth with Tax Efficiency

When it comes to building wealth for retirement, people often dream about the possibility of paying no taxes in their golden years. But let's get real: The idea of paying *zero* taxes in retirement isn't likely—unless you have nothing to live on. While there are plenty of strategies to *reduce* your tax burden and make your money last longer, taxes will always be part of the equation. The key is to focus on tax efficiency: minimizing the taxes you pay while maximizing your investment returns.

In this chapter, we'll explore the importance of understanding how taxes work in retirement and the strategies you can use to reduce your tax liability. From choosing the right investment accounts to timing your withdrawals, we'll cover how to be smart about taxes without falling for the myth that you can completely avoid them.

### Why Taxes Still Matter in Retirement

Many people enter retirement expecting their tax burden to shrink significantly. While you may not pay as much in taxes as you did during your working years, your taxes are not

> Tax diversification is one of the best ways to manage your tax liability in retirement. You can make withdrawals in a tax-efficient way, pulling from the most advantageous accounts based on your financial situation each year.

going away. In fact, in some cases your tax situation can become even more complex. Between income taxes, capital gains taxes, and taxes on Social Security benefits, it's important to plan ahead to avoid surprises.

If you've been saving in a traditional 401(k) or IRA, you've been deferring taxes on both your contributions and the growth in those accounts. In retirement, when you start withdrawing from these accounts, you'll pay ordinary income tax on every dollar you take out. And as of 2024, once you reach age 73, you're required to start taking Required Minimum Distributions (RMDs), whether you need the money or not.

Many people are surprised to learn that their Social Security benefits might be taxable. If your combined income (which includes half of your Social Security benefits plus any other retirement income) exceeds a certain threshold, you could be taxed on up to 85% of your benefits.

If you've invested in taxable brokerage accounts, you'll be subject to capital gains taxes when you sell investments. Short-term capital gains (on assets held for less than a year) are taxed at your ordinary income rate, while long-term capital gains (on assets held for more than a year) benefit from lower tax rates. Still, those gains can add up, so it's important to be strategic about when and how you sell.

If you're lucky enough to have a pension or other forms of retirement income, you'll be taxed on that income at your ordinary income rate.

## Strategies for Tax Efficiency in Retirement

While you can't eliminate taxes, you *can* reduce their impact by being strategic about how you manage your accounts, withdrawals, and investments. One of the most powerful tools for tax efficiency is choosing the right accounts for your savings. Tax-advantaged accounts allow you to defer or even eliminate taxes on your savings, depending on the type of account. The two main types of tax-advantaged retirement accounts are tax-deferred and tax-free.

With tax-deferred accounts such as a traditional 401(k) or a traditional IRA, you contribute pre-tax dollars, meaning you don't pay taxes on the money now. Instead, your contributions grow tax-free until you withdraw them in retirement, at which point they are taxed as ordinary income.

Tax-free accounts such as the Roth 401(k) or Roth IRA allow you to contribute after-tax dollars, meaning you've already paid taxes on the money before it goes into the account. The big benefit? In retirement, all withdrawals—both your contributions and the growth—are completely tax-free.

One powerful strategy is converting traditional IRA or 401(k) funds to a Roth IRA. By paying taxes on the converted amount now, you can grow those assets tax-free and enjoy tax-free withdrawals in retirement. This strategy can be particularly effective in years when you have lower income and are in a lower tax bracket.

In your taxable brokerage accounts, you do pay taxes on interest, dividends, and capital gains along the way, but you are not taxed when withdrawing your principal.

Tax diversification is one of the best ways to manage your tax liability in retirement. By spreading your savings across different types of accounts (tax-deferred, tax-free, and taxable), you'll have more control over your tax situation when you retire. This gives you the flexibility to withdraw from different accounts depending on your needs and tax bracket each year.

By having a mix of these accounts, you can make withdrawals in a tax-efficient way, pulling from the most advantageous accounts based on your financial situation each year.

Timing is everything when it comes to withdrawals in retirement. You can control your tax liability by being thoughtful about when and how much you withdraw from each type of account.

If possible, delaying Social Security until full retirement age (or later) not only increases your monthly benefits but also gives you more time to withdraw from tax-deferred accounts at potentially lower tax rates.

Starting at age 73, you'll be required to take Required Minimum Distributions from your tax-deferred accounts. If you don't need the income, consider making Qualified Charitable Distributions (QCDs) to donate directly to charity and avoid paying taxes on the amount.

And you always want to  be mindful of capital gains when selling investments. If you have losing investments, you can sell them to offset gains in other parts of your portfolio, a strategy known as tax-loss harvesting.

The reality is that unless you have very little income or savings, taxes will be part of your retirement. The goal isn't to avoid taxes entirely—it's to manage them in a way that preserves your wealth while keeping your tax bill as low as possible. Remember, the promise of a tax-free retirement is often unrealistic. If anyone says they can help you pay *zero* taxes in retirement, ask what you'll be living on with their plan—because paying no taxes typically means you don't have much income to tax in the first place.

### Training Takeaway: Embrace Tax Efficiency, Not Tax Avoidance

At the end of the day, paying taxes is part of life—and part of retirement. But by embracing tax efficiency, you can keep your tax bill under control while still maintaining a healthy income in retirement. Remember that smart tax strategies aren't about avoiding taxes altogether; they're about making the most of the tax advantages available to you while still building and protecting your wealth.

As you approach retirement, work with a financial planner to create a tax-efficient withdrawal strategy that balances your income needs with your long-term goals. Taxes may not go away, but with the right planning, you can keep more of your money working for you.

MELISSA COX, CFP®

## Leveraging Technology for Financial Management

Let's be real—technology has totally changed the way we handle money. With a few taps, you can invest, budget, and have a robot manage your entire portfolio while you binge-watch your favorite shows. Tech tools have made managing finances more accessible, and probably even a bit more fun.

But while algorithms and apps make life easier, they lack that special human touch. Financial decisions aren't always cut-and-dry, and as smart as technology is, it can't sip a coffee with you and understand your life's nuances. So while technology is a fantastic sidekick, the hero of your financial story is a blend of human insight and tech savvy. In this chapter, we'll explore how to get the best of both worlds.

### The Benefits of Digital Financial Tools

Technology isn't just for selfies and online shopping—there are tons of apps and platforms out there making money management simpler than ever. With apps like RocketMoney, YNAB, and EveryDollar, you can track every penny, set financial goals, and get notifications when you're a little too swipe-happy at your favorite coffee shop.

Platforms like Robinhood and Acorns have made it easier than ever to start investing—even with just pocket change. Fancy apps that round up your purchases into micro-investments? Yep, that's a thing now. And for the more seasoned investors, platforms like Vanguard and Fidelity offer all the bells and whistles.

Tired of picking stocks or don't have time to obsess over market trends? Platforms like Betterment and Wealthfront are well-known in this space, but major investment firms such as Vanguard and Fidelity also offer robo-advisory services. Vanguard's Digital Advisor and Fidelity Go provide automated portfolio management tailored to your financial goals and risk tolerance. They build, balance, and manage your portfolio based on your goals and risk tolerance, making investing as simple as ordering takeout.

While robo-advisors offer convenience and low fees, they may not provide the personalized guidance that a human financial advisor can offer. If you prefer a more customized approach, consider working with a Certified Financial Planner™ who can tailor strategies to your unique situation. However, it's important to note that many financial advisors also utilize algorithmic tools to enhance their services, so completely avoiding automated assistance is increasingly uncommon in today's investment landscape.

While tech tools are amazing, they have their limits. Relying only on robo-advisors can be like using a GPS without looking at the road—you might end up in a ditch without even realizing it. Robo-advisors are great for basic goals, but they're not going to know that you're planning to sell a business or expecting an inheritance. A human advisor can look at your whole financial picture—family, goals, and all—to help you make more nuanced decisions.

Robo-advisors often overlook the finer points of bond trading. Meanwhile, human advisors can take advantage of bond market quirks, like buying bonds at a discount or capitalizing on timing that algorithms just don't catch.

And, of course, robo-advisors and apps aren't immune to technical glitches. You know the feeling when your favorite streaming service crashes in the middle of the best part? Now imagine that happening to your investment platform. Even the best platforms aren't perfect. A technical hiccup can mess up a trade or miscalculate a rebalance. No big deal, unless it happens during a market swing. Yikes. And if your platform crashes during a major market move, you could miss key trades and opportunities.

With great money comes great responsibility—and also hackers. While platforms are designed to be secure, they aren't bulletproof. Breaches happen, and getting your info back in order after an attack can be a protracted pain.

Algorithms make decisions based on rules, but sometimes the real world throws a wrench in those rules. A robo-advisor might rebalance your portfolio in the middle of market chaos, but a human advisor might take a step back and assess before acting.

### Balancing Technology with Human Insight

So how do you get the most out of tech without losing the human touch? Balance, my friends.

Let tech handle the routine stuff. Apps are great for

automating the day-to-day—budgeting, saving, and even rebalancing investments. Let them handle the boring parts while you enjoy the peace of mind knowing your finances are in order. But you want to call in the humans for big decisions. When it comes to major life events—retirement, buying a house, starting a business—nothing beats a human advisor. They can see the bigger picture and help you navigate tricky situations that robo-advisors just aren't equipped to handle.

Markets are unpredictable, and a human advisor can help adjust your financial plan in real time. When the market goes haywire, human advisors are available to keep you from making emotional decisions by asking probing questions and offering thoughtful solutions.

### Training Takeaway: Technology and Human Advisors— A Winning Combination

Technology and human insight don't have to compete—they can work together. Let apps streamline your finances, but keep a human advisor in your corner for the big stuff. Combining the efficiency of tech with the wisdom of human expertise is the best way to build a financial plan that's resilient, flexible, and future-focused.

MELISSA COX, CFP®

## Sustainable Investing—
## Aligning Financial Goals with Values

The way people invest has evolved. More and more investors are aiming to grow their wealth while also aligning their investments with their personal values. Whether it's saving the planet, advocating for social justice, or just making sure their dollars don't end up funding the next corporate fraud, investors are realizing that financial success and doing good can go hand in hand. Enter sustainable investing, also known as ESG investing (Environmental, Social, and Governance)— because you can make money *and* make a difference.

### What Is Sustainable Investing?

At its core, sustainable investing is about more than just returns. You're not just thinking about how much money you'll earn—you're also asking, "How's this company treating the planet? Their employees? Their board members?" It's a holistic approach that looks beyond the bottom line. These investors typically ask themselves all or some of the following questions before deciding to invest in a particular company:

- Does the company care about the planet, or are they basically setting fire to the rainforest?
- Do they reduce carbon emissions, conserve resources, or adopt sustainable practices?
- How does the company treat people? This includes labor practices, diversity and inclusion, and community engagement.
- Is the company run responsibly?
- Are leadership and board members being compensated fairly, and do they follow ethical business practices?

In other words, you're investing in companies that *walk the talk*. You don't have to choose between making money and doing good—you can do both, and that's where sustainable investing shines.

Over the past decade, ESG investing has gone from a niche strategy to a mainstream option. What's behind the rise? Millennials and Gen Z are all about making the world a better place, and they want their investments to reflect that ideology. When generations with buying power start talking, the market listens.

Companies know people are paying attention, so they've started setting real goals—whether it's reducing carbon emissions or upping the diversity in their C-suite. It's a win-win: Investors get more choices,

## Environmental, Social, and Governance (ESG) Investing

An investment approach that considers a company's performance and impact in areas like environmental sustainability, social responsibility, and ethical governance. It aims to align financial goals with values.

and companies look good for being responsible.

Research shows that companies with strong ESG practices often have lower risks and better long-term growth prospects. Why? Companies that take care of the environment and their employees tend to have fewer lawsuits, lower regulatory hurdles, and more productive workforces.

## How to Start ESG Investing and Sustainable ESG Strategies

If you think you want to implement some ESG investing, start by asking yourself what really matters to you. Whether it's fighting climate change, fair labor, or ethical leadership, once you know your values, you can invest in companies that match them.

Sites like Morningstar, MSCI, and Sustainalytics offer ESG ratings, so you can see how companies perform on sustainability metrics. Think of it as Yelp for companies' values. If you don't want to research individual companies, ESG mutual funds and ETFs have already done the heavy lifting for you. They're diversified and focus on sustainability, making it easy to invest with your conscience intact.

But don't forget about the rest of your portfolio. Diversification helps manage risk, and ESG funds offer plenty of options so that you're not putting all your green eggs in one basket.

Depending on your goals and how actively you want to manage your investments, there are several strategies you can use for ESG. First, you can simply just not invest in companies you don't agree with. You can cut out industries like tobacco, oil, or weapons, keeping your portfolio "sin-free." Or you can actively choose companies that lead the charge on ESG factors. It's about rewarding businesses that make a positive impact. If you want to take it a step further, you can put money into companies and projects that are driving change—like clean water technologies or affordable housing.

Sustainable investing isn't a flash in the pan. As environmental challenges, social justice movements, and corporate accountability become more central, more investors are hopping on the ESG bandwagon. It's a shift in thinking—where financial success is aligned with improving the world around us.

### Training Takeaway: Aligning Profit with Purpose

Sustainable investing is about more than just making money—it's also about making a difference. By incorporating ESG criteria into your investment strategy, you can align your financial goals with your personal values helping to build a future that benefits both you and the world around you. Whether you're passionate about the environment, social justice, or ethical corporate governance, there's an investment strategy that can help you achieve your financial goals while staying true to your values.

The key is finding the right balance between feeling good about where your money goes and making sure your investments are as healthy as your conscience. After all, it's all about profit with a purpose--and having at least a little fun along the way.

MELISSA COX, CFP®

# Protecting

## Insurance: Demystifying Life Insurance

Life loves to throw curveballs. Markets fluctuate, accidents happen, and the unexpected often shows up at the worst possible time. While diversification and smart investing provide a strong defense, insurance is your backup plan—a safety net designed to protect everything you've worked so hard to build. Let's dive into the types of insurance every financial plan should include to ensure your wealth is protected from life's uncertainties.

While investing builds wealth, insurance ensures that your financial foundation remains intact when the unexpected happens. Think of insurance as the unsung hero of financial planning—it's there when you need it most, providing stability during turbulent times

Let's start with the big one: *life insurance*. It's not exactly a fun topic, but it's crucial for protecting your family. Think of it as your way of looking after your loved ones, even if you're not alive.

Life insurance covers everything from funeral costs to mortgage payments, ensuring your family isn't left scrambling. Whether you're in the early stages of building a family,

MELISSA COX, CFP®

growing your wealth, or preparing for retirement, life insurance plays a critical role in securing your financial legacy.

### Term vs. Permanent Insurance: The Great Debate

Ah, the term vs. permanent insurance debate. It's an argument that could rival the endless "renting vs. owning" discussions. But before the pitchforks come out, let's come to terms with one thing: They're both okay. Really. They both have their place in your financial plan—it just depends on your needs.

Term insurance is like renting. You're covered for a specific period (usually 10, 20, or 30 years), and it's typically the most affordable option. If something happens to you during the term, your beneficiaries get the payout. But once the term is up, that's it—no more coverage. If you outlive your policy, there's no payout, and you'll need to get a new policy if you still want coverage.

Permanent insurance, on the other hand, is like owning your home. It covers you for your entire life (as long as you pay your premiums), and it builds cash value over time. This cash value can be borrowed against or used for other purposes. Permanent insurance comes in different forms, like Whole Life and Indexed Universal Life (IUL), but we'll dive into those in a minute.

Let's dive deeper into permanent insurance and its cash-value component. With a permanent life insurance policy, you not only get lifelong coverage but also the ability to build up cash value that you can access while you're still alive. This is where things get interesting and a little more complicated.

Whole Life Insurance is the traditional form of permanent insurance. It provides a death benefit, guaranteed, and builds cash value over time at a set interest rate. This makes it a stable option, but it usually is more expensive than term insurance.

Indexed Universal Life (IUL) is a more modern option. It of-

> ### Indexed Universal Life Insurance (IUL)
>
> A type of permanent life insurance that combines a death benefit with a cash value component tied to the performance of a stock market index, such as the S&P 500. It offers flexible premiums, potential for cash value growth, and downside protection through guaranteed minimum interest rates.

fers the potential for cash value growth tied to a market index (like the S&P 500). You're not directly investing in the market, but your cash value can grow based on how the index performs, giving you a little more upside potential. It's kind of like a choose-your-own-adventure book for your insurance policy—the potential for growth is there, but it comes with a little more risk.

And yes, if you ever need to access that money, you can borrow against the cash value in your policy, often tax-free. But here's the catch: If you borrow too much and don't repay it, you could reduce the death benefit or even risk the policy lapsing. So while cash value policies can be a great financial tool, they're not the miracles they're sometimes made out to be.

MELISSA COX, CFP®

So which one is better? That depends on your needs. If you're looking for affordable coverage to protect your family while paying off a mortgage or raising kids, term insurance might be enough. But if you want something with more flexibility and with the potential for long-term benefits, permanent insurance could be the way to go. Of course, your insurance needs are going to change over the years, so you can start with what you can afford and layer in more coverage as needed.

One of the biggest concerns with life insurance—and long-term care (LTC) policies—is the risk of premium increases over time. Some older whole life and universal life policies and traditional LTC policies have premiums that can jump significantly as you age or if the policy costs outpace expectations. This can put a financial strain on policyholders down the road.

However, many modern Indexed Universal Life (IUL) policies are now designed with level premiums that are intended not to increase unless you've opted for a specific design feature like flexible premiums or overfunding options. Traditional LTC policies, on the other hand, are still prone to premium increases as healthcare costs rise and policyholders get older. In contrast, hybrid life insurance policies with LTC riders generally have more predictable premiums since they combine the death benefit with long-term care coverage.

## Long-Term Care Insurance (LTC)

Covers expenses for nursing homes, assisted living, or in-home care, reducing the financial burden of extended care needs.

When evaluating life or LTC insurance, it's critical to understand how premiums work over time, especially since increasing premiums could impact your ability to maintain coverage when you need it most.

### Riders: The Extra Protection You Didn't Know You Needed

Life-insurance riders are like add-ons that you can attach to your policy for extra protection. Some of the most common:

- **Waiver of Premium Rider**. If you become disabled and can't work, this rider will cover your premiums, keeping your policy in force without you having to pay for it.
- **Accidental Death Benefit**: This rider provides an additional payout if you die in an accident, often doubling the policy's benefit.
- **Disability Income Rider**: If you're unable to work due to a disability, this rider provides income to help replace what you've lost.
- **Long-Term Care (LTC) Rider**: This one is particularly important as we'll discuss in a moment. It allows you to tap into your death benefit early if you need to pay for long-term care expenses.

Riders add flexibility to your policy, but they also come with additional costs. Make sure the extra protection aligns with your overall financial goals before adding too many.

### Life Insurance:
### Modern Uses for Disability and Long-Term Care

Here's where life insurance has really evolved: Modern life insurance policies are no longer just about covering funeral costs. They now offer options for long-term care and disability.

MELISSA COX, CFP®

And let's be honest—long-term care is expensive. A traditional LTC policy can be monumentally costly, and worst of all, it's a "use it or lose it" situation. If you never need long-term care, all those premiums are essentially gone.

That's where hybrid life insurance policies come in. These policies combine life insurance with long-term care benefits, giving you a two-in-one solution. If you need long-term care, you can tap into the policy's death benefit to cover the costs. If you don't end up needing LTC, your beneficiaries still get the payout when you pass away. It's a win-win because it eliminates the "use it or lose it" nature of traditional LTC policies.

Hybrid policies typically start paying once you can't perform two out of six activities of daily living (ADLs), like bathing or dressing. And unlike traditional LTC policies that reimburse you for care, hybrid policies often start paying right away without the 90-day waiting period you'd face with standalone LTC insurance. That flexibility can make a huge difference when you need care quickly.

While life insurance is a valuable financial tool, it's not without its pitfalls. One of the most common issues people face is overcomplicated policy design. Life insurance policies can be simple, or they can rival the blueprints of a skyscraper—and sometimes the Leaning Tower of Pisa if they're not done right. Be wary of overly complex policies that are hard to understand. And watch out for pushy salespeople who try to sell life insurance as the solution to all your financial problems. Some may promise that an insurance policy will replace any need for traditional savings or investing. That's simply not true. Life insurance is *one piece* of your financial puzzle, but it shouldn't replace sound investment strategies or your retirement plan. Work with a Certified Financial Planner™ who can guide you through your options.

### Training Takeaway: Regular Reviews Matter

What worked for you 10 years ago may not fit your life today. As your financial goals evolve, your life insurance should, too. Older policies might become defunct as time marches on, and you may find they no longer meet your needs. This is where working with a CFP® comes in handy. They can help you stay on top of your policies and ensure they're aligned with your family's financial future.

# Property / Asset Insurance

One often overlooked part of financial protection is property and casualty insurance. This includes homeowner's insurance, renter's insurance, and auto insurance. These policies cover your assets and protect you from life's unpredictable moments, like fires, accidents, or theft. The right policy ensures that if something happens to your home or car, you aren't left footing the entire bill.

Here are some types of insurance to consider, depending on your personal situation:

- **Homeowner's Insurance.** Whether you own a house or a condo, this insurance covers the structure and belongings inside. It also protects against liability if someone gets injured on your property. Without it, a disaster like a house fire could be financially devastating.

- **Renter's Insurance.** If you're renting, this insurance protects your personal belongings from theft or damage and also provides liability coverage. It's an affordable way to ensure your possessions are covered in case of an unexpected event.

- **Landlord Insurance.** For those who own rental properties, this specialized insurance protects the structure and may offer liability coverage if tenants or visitors are injured on the property.

- **Auto Insurance**. Required by law in most places, auto insurance protects you from the financial impact of car accidents, whether it's damage to your vehicle or to someone else's.
- **Damage to Your Vehicle.** Repairs or replacement after an accident, theft, or other covered incidents.
- **Liability Coverage:** If you're at fault, it pays for damage to others' property or vehicles.
- **Medical Expenses:** Many policies include coverage for healthcare costs for injuries to you, your passengers, or others involved in an accident, depending on the policy and coverage options.

Having the right coverage can mean the difference between a minor inconvenience and a financial disaster. Make sure your property and assets are insured properly to avoid any big surprises down the road.

### Umbrella Insurance: Extra Coverage for the Unexpected

Umbrella insurance is an extra layer of protection that kicks in when your other insurance policies (like homeowner's or auto) reach their limits. Say you're involved in a serious car accident, and the damages exceed your auto insurance coverage. That's where umbrella insurance steps in, covering the excess and preventing you from paying out of pocket.

Umbrella insurance is relatively inexpensive for the amount of protection it provides. It's especially important for people with significant assets—like a home, savings, or investments—to make sure those assets aren't at risk if a major liability arises.

MELISSA COX, CFP®

### Business Insurance and E&O Insurance

If you own a business or work in a field where professional liability is a concern, business insurance and Errors & Omissions (E&O) insurance are essential. Business insurance protects your company's property, equipment, and even liability against lawsuits. It's especially important for small business owners who might not have the resources to recover from a significant financial loss.

E&O insurance covers professional mistakes that could lead to lawsuits. For example, if you provide financial advice, legal services, or any other professional service, E&O insurance ensures that a mistake doesn't jeopardize your personal finances or your business. It protects professionals against claims of negligence or failure to perform duties that result in financial harm to a client. It's crucial in fields like finance, legal, or medical where even small mistakes can lead to significant lawsuits.

### Training Takeaway: Prepare for the Unexpected

We can't predict the future, but we can prepare for it. Protecting your portfolio from risk isn't just about surviving tough times—it's also about thriving in the long run. By setting up the right insurance and covering yourself for those unexpected twists, you're setting yourself up for financial success no matter what comes your way.

On the other hand, after going through all the different types of insurance, you might feel like you've been covered with a pile of coats—one for every possible risk out there. And while it's comforting to know you're protected, being over-insured can be a risk in itself. Just like you wouldn't want to wear five layers on a sunny day, too much insurance can weigh you down financially. That's why working with a professional to help you find the right balance is just as important. The goal is to be prepared, but not suffocated by unnecessary premiums.

Managing risk is all about peace of mind—so that no matter what happens, you know your financial future is secure, and you're free to focus on what matters most without feeling buried under all that coverage!

MELISSA COX, CFP®

## Decoding Health Insurance:
## Coverage, Costs, and Common Surprises

Health insurance.

Just saying the words out loud might make you groan. It's that rite of passage no one ever really masters. You finally feel like you've got it all figured out, and then—bam!—your coverage changes, your deductible resets, or you get a surprise bill for something you thought was covered.

Health insurance can make even the most financially savvy individuals want to throw their hands up and shout, "How does anyone actually understand this?"

But don't worry, we're going to break it down—because while health insurance may feel like a never-ending riddle, understanding the basics will help you make better financial decisions. Spoiler alert: There's no magic wand that'll make health insurance easy, but by the end of this chapter, you should know the basics.

### The Basics: How Health Insurance Works

Health insurance is essentially a contract between you and an insurance company. You pay a premium every month, and in exchange, the insurance company agrees to help cover some of your medical expenses. Simple, right? Not so fast. There's fine print—lots of it—and navigating that fine print is where things get tricky.

There are a few key terms you need to know:

- **Premium.** This is the amount you pay every month to keep your insurance active, kind of like a subscription to Netflix. Except it doesn't come with a bingeable series; it comes with access to healthcare (and probably some headaches).

- **Deductible.** This is the amount you have to pay out of pocket each year before your insurance kicks in. Think of it as a cover charge before the insurance company starts picking up the tab. Until you hit your deductible, most costs are on you.

- **Copayment (Copay).** This is a fixed amount you pay for a covered healthcare service, like a doctor's visit or a prescription. It's like paying for parking at the hospital—annoying but necessary.

- **Coinsurance.** After you've met your deductible, you still have to share some of the costs with your insurance company. This is where coinsurance comes in. For example, if your plan covers 80% of a service, you'll be responsible for the remaining 20%. Don't celebrate when you meet your deductible too soon—coinsurance will still keep you on the hook.

- **Out-of-Pocket Maximum.** This is the most you'll have to pay in one year for covered services. Once you hit this limit, your insurance covers 100% of everything for the rest of the year. It's like reaching the summit of a very expensive mountain—once you're there, it's a smooth ride down—at least until the next year!

MELISSA COX, CFP®

## What's Covered?

One of the most frustrating aspects of health insurance is figuring out what's actually covered by your policy. Your coverage depends on the type of plan you have, whether it's a Health Maintenance Organization (HMO), Preferred Provider Organization (PPO), or something else entirely:

- **HMO**: This type of plan requires you to see doctors within a specific network. If you venture outside of that network, it's like trying to use an expired coupon—your insurance won't cover it unless it's an emergency. HMOs often have lower premiums and deductibles, but they also come with fewer choices.
- **PPO**: With a PPO, you can see any doctor you want, but you'll pay more if you go out of network. It's like having a VIP pass that gets you access to more providers but at a higher cost.
- **High Deductible Health Plan (HDHP)**: This plan comes with a higher deductible but lower monthly premiums. HDHPs are often paired with Health Savings Accounts (HSAs) letting you save pre-tax dollars to use for medical expenses. Think of an HSA as a health-focused piggy bank you can tap into when needed.

> Sometimes, figuring out what your health insurance covers and what it doesn't can feel like a stab in the dark. But you can figure it out—and you must.

Sometimes, figuring out what's covered and what isn't can feel like a stab in the dark. Your plan might cover preventive care (yay, free flu shots!), but when it comes to that specialist you really need to see? Maybe not. And let's not forget about prescription drugs. Insurance formularies (the list of drugs they cover) are like a shifting labyrinth—your specific medicine could be fully covered one year and completely off the list the next.

### How to Navigate the Health Insurance Maze

Health insurance can be confusing, but here are a few strategies to help you avoid some of the pitfalls:

- **Read Your Plan Documents**. I know, I know—who has time to read pages of insurance jargon? But understanding the basics of your plan's coverage, including deductibles, copays, and which providers are in-network, can save you from surprise bills later.
- **Stay In-Network**. Whenever possible, stick to in-network providers. Going out of network can result in massive bills that insurance won't cover, and nobody wants to spend their Saturday afternoon trying to negotiate a $5,000 bill for a 20-minute consultation.
- **Get a Cost Estimate**. Before non-emergency procedures, request a cost estimate from your insurer. Most can provide detailed estimates to help you budget for surgical needs.
- **Max Out Your Benefits**. If you have health needs that require a lot of doctor visits or treatments, aim to hit your out-of-pocket maximum early in the year. Once you hit it, your insurance will cover 100% of everything else. It's like a free-for-all—but only after you've paid enough to make you cry.

MELISSA COX, CFP®

- **Use Preventive Care**. Most insurance plans cover preventive care like vaccines, screenings, and annual checkups for free. Take advantage of these services because staying on top of your health can prevent bigger and more expensive problems down the road.

### The Wild Card: Surprise Bills and Coverage Gaps

Even if you do everything right, health insurance can still surprise you—and not in a good way. Surprise bills happen when you receive care from an out-of-network provider without realizing it. For example, you might go to an in-network hospital for surgery, only to find out later that the anesthesiologist wasn't in-network. Boom—surprise bill!

Let's look at an example of how coverage might work for a family of four. Imagine you met your family's $6,000 deductible early in the year (maybe someone had surgery or a series of doctor visits). Great, right? Now your insurance should cover 80-90% of your future medical costs until you hit your out-of-pocket maximum (let's say that's $10,000 for the year).

Now fast forward to the first snow day of the year. As you're outside admiring the snowfall and keeping the kids from throwing snowballs inside the house, mom slips on the ice, breaking her wrist. She needs surgery to fix it. What happens next?

The ER visit, X-rays, surgery, and follow-up care might cost $10,000. Normally, that would be a major hit. But since you've already met your deductible, your insurance will cover 80% of the cost, leaving you with $2,000 to pay (that's your 20% coinsurance).

Depending on the other medical bills you've racked up over

the year, this new expense might push you close to your out-of-pocket maximum. If this event pushes you over the $10,000 out-of-pocket max, your insurance will cover 100% of any additional medical expenses for the rest of the year.

So while mom's broken wrist and surgery might feel like a holiday disaster, at least financially, the blow is softened because your insurance picks up the rest once you've hit your deductible and out-of-pocket max.

Pro Tip: Always be aware of where you stand in relation to your deductible and out-of-pocket maximum. It can help you plan for unexpected health expenses and minimize surprises.

### Training Takeaway:
### Mastering Health Insurance Basics for Peace of Mind

Health insurance is a necessary evil, but it doesn't have to be an overwhelming one. By understanding the basic terms, sticking to in-network providers, and taking full advantage of your plan's preventive care options, you can make health insurance work for you and your wallet. Navigating health insurance will always feel a bit like fumbling in the dark. But with the right strategies in place, you can minimize the guesswork and avoid the worst surprises. And who knows? You might even get through a year without any unexpected bills.

MELISSA COX, CFP®

## Navigating Social Security and Medicare

When it comes to retirement, everyone loves to talk about Social Security and Medicare like they're the ultimate safety nets. And while they do provide important benefits, there's a catch—Social Security was never designed to be your *sole* source of retirement income. Think of it more like the icing on the retirement cake, not the cake itself. Over time, it's possible that Social Security could become means-tested—meaning even if you've been diligent and saved well, you might see less of that icing than others.

In this chapter, we'll break down what Social Security and Medicare really offer, how you can maximize your benefits, and what you need to know about their limitations. Plus, a reality check: When I'm working with clients, I try not to count on Social Security unless they're nearing retirement age. We all hope it will be there, but it's tricky to predict in what form—or how much icing—will be left for everyone else down the road.

### Social Security: The Backup Plan, Not the Main Show

First things first: Picture Social Security like the backup

band at a concert—
it's there to add a lit-
tle extra, but it's not
the star of the show.
The problem is, many
people assume Social
Security will take care
of everything in re-
tirement—from gro-
ceries to medical bills
to vacations. Spoiler
alert: It will not.

Right now, the
average Social Secu-
rity benefit is around

> Social Security is far from enough to cover all your expenses. That's why you also need savings, investments, or even pension income to truly enjoy your retirement years.

$1,800 a month. And while that sounds like a nice bit of cash, it's far from enough to cover all your expenses, especially once you factor in housing, healthcare, and those extra "I'm retired now" hobbies. This is why you need more than just Social Security—you need savings, investments, or even pension income to truly enjoy your retirement years.

And here's the kicker: There's no guarantee that Social Security will stay the same in the future. We've already heard the rumblings about means testing—basically, the more you've saved, the less Social Security you may get. The idea is to direct more benefits to those who need it most. So if you've been a superstar at saving for retirement (which I hope you are), you might not see the same benefits as someone who hasn't saved a dime.

That's why, especially with younger clients, I tend to err on the side of caution and not rely too much on Social Security.

MELISSA COX, CFP®

Sure, we hope it'll be there, but we just don't know what form it will take.

## Maximizing Your Social Security Benefits

Even though Social Security won't cover everything, it's still money in your pocket, and I'm all about helping you maximize it. So let's talk about how you can get the most out of it.

- **Know your full retirement age (FRA).** Your Full Retirement Age is the magic number when it comes to Social Security. It's the age at which you can start receiving 100% of your benefits. For most people, this age is somewhere between 66 and 67. Claim your benefits before that, and you'll take a hit—and who wants that? Wait longer, and you'll get more.

- **Delay benefits for a bigger payoff.** If you can afford to wait, delaying your Social Security benefits past your FRA can be one of the best moves you make. For every year you delay after your FRA, your monthly benefits increase by about 8%. That's like getting a raise just for being patient. The trick is making sure you don't need the money right away. But if you can hold off until 70, you'll have a much bigger monthly check—kind of like getting an extra scoop of that icing. However, if you're not in the best health or have a shorter life expectancy based on family history, claiming earlier might be the smart move.

- **Don't forget spousal benefits.** If you're married, spousal benefits can provide an additional boost to your Social Security income. You can claim up to 50% of your spouse's Social Security benefit if your own benefit is smaller than that amount. This ensures you're not penalized for earning less or spending time out of the workforce. If your spouse is claiming 100% of their earned Social Security benefit, you can still claim a spousal benefit of up to 50% of their amount, provided you meet the eligibility criteria. However, this applies only if your own benefit is less than 50% of your spouse's. Essentially, you receive whichever benefit is higher—your own or the spousal benefit—but not both. If you're claiming a spousal benefit, it doesn't reduce the amount your spouse receives. It's an additional benefit provided by Social Security.

## What Happens to Your Social Security Benefits When You Die?

When a Social Security beneficiary passes away, their benefits don't simply vanish. Certain family members—such as a surviving spouse, minor children, or disabled dependents—may be eligible for survivor benefits. If you were the higher earner, your surviving spouse could receive your benefit instead of their own, but they won't get both.

The surviving spouse can collect the full benefit if they've reached full retirement age or a reduced amount if they're younger. Minor children can also qualify for a portion of the benefits until they turn 18 (or 19, if still in school).

And here's a fun (or possibly awkward) detail: If you've been married before, your ex-spouse may be eligible for part of your benefit as long as the marriage lasted at least 10 years. So, it's possible that your ex-spouse could collect a portion of your benefits while your surviving spouse receives theirs—the ex truly is the gift that keeps on giving! To ensure your loved

MELISSA COX, CFP®

ones receive what they're entitled to, it's important to contact the Social Security Administration after a death.

### Medicare: What You Need to Know About Healthcare in Retirement

Now, let's switch gears to Medicare, the other big piece of the retirement puzzle. While Social Security is about income, Medicare is about healthcare—and in retirement, healthcare can be a huge expense. Like Social Security, Medicare is a bit more complicated than just signing up and calling it a day.

Medicare comes in different parts, and understanding how they work is key:

- **Medicare Part A.** This covers hospital stays, skilled nursing facilities, and some home healthcare. If you've worked long enough, you won't pay any premium for Part A. Think of this as your hospital safety net.
- **Medicare Part B.** This covers outpatient services like doctor visits, preventive care, and medical equipment. You'll pay a premium for Part B, and that amount depends on your income.
- **Medicare Part C** (Medicare Advantage). Medicare Advantage plans are offered by private insurers and bundle Parts A (hospital insurance) and B (medical insurance) into one plan, often throwing in extras like vision, dental, and hearing coverage. Think of it as the "deluxe package" of Medicare. However, there's a trade-off: Medicare Advantage plans typically require you to stay within their network of doctors and hospitals to get full benefits which can limit your choices. In contrast, traditional Medicare combined with a Medicare Supplement (Medigap) plan offers more

flexibility, allowing you to see any doctor or specialist nationwide who accepts Medicare—no network restrictions. The choice between Medicare Advantage and traditional Medicare plus Medigap often comes down to balancing cost, convenience, and the freedom to choose your healthcare providers

- **Medicare Part D**. Prescription drug coverage which you can add to traditional Medicare or sometimes get through Medicare Advantage.

### Training Takeaway: Hope for the Best, Plan for the Worst

Here's the thing with Social Security and Medicare: It's great to have them as part of your plan, but they shouldn't be your entire plan. The reality is, we don't know exactly what Social Security will look like in the future or how Medicare might change. So my advice is to hope for the best, but plan for the worst.

Social Security should be a slice of your retirement income, but you'll need other layers (savings, investments, or pensions) to truly feel comfortable. And when it comes to Medicare, don't forget about the gaps in coverage—because those gaps could surprise you if you're not prepared.

MELISSA COX, CFP®

## Family Finances:
## The Importance of Communication

Money can be a tricky subject for families to talk about. For some, it's awkward and uncomfortable, while for others, it's a ticking time bomb just waiting to go off. But here's the thing—*not* talking about money is one of the fastest ways to derail a family's financial future. Miscommunication (or no communication at all) can lead to poor decisions, missed opportunities, and even long-term financial instability. And let's be honest, the last thing you want is for your family to bicker over dollars and cents. What you do want is to keep everyone on the same page without losing your mind.

### How Miscommunication Can Blow Up a Family's Finances

Ever heard of the phrase "too many cooks in the kitchen spoil the broth?" Well, the same applies to finances. Except in this case, the problem usually isn't too many cooks, but cooks who don't even know what recipe they're following.

A family may have financial goals, but when no one is talking, assumptions take over. One person thinks they're saving for retirement, while the other is splurging on a surprise renovation. And suddenly, everyone's scratching their heads, wondering why there's no money left for that summer vacation.

The thing is, it's not just about the money—it's about expectations. When everyone's not on the same page, chaos ensues. You might think your spouse knows you're saving for an emergency fund, but they're daydreaming about a new car. Or maybe you've told your kids you'll cover their college costs, but they think you're secretly sitting on a trust fund. Financial miscommunication leads to unnecessary arguments and more than a little drama. Or worse.

> Scams are a great example of poor communication leading to poor bank accounts. And let's be real, scams aren't just a problem for Grandma and Grandpa anymore.

Scams are a great example of poor communication leading to poor bank accounts. And let's be real, scams aren't just a problem for Grandma and Grandpa anymore. Sure, older generations are often targeted by scammers offering too-good-to-be-true investments or pretending to be the IRS needing your Social Security number on a phone call. (Just to be clear, the real IRS will *never* do that. And don't ever give your Social Security number to *anyone* who calls you.) But young people aren't immune from scams either. From phishing emails, to online investment schemes, scams are lurking around every corner, and they're getting harder to spot.

MELISSA COX, CFP®

Here's the kicker: Without good communication, families often don't realize someone's been scammed until it's too late. Grandma might be too embarrassed to admit she gave her credit card number to a fake customer service rep, and your tech-savvy nephew might not think twice about dumping money into a cryptocurrency scam.

The reality is, scams are evolving, and by the time someone figures it out, the money's long gone. This is why regular conversations about finances are key—talking about common scams, red flags, and how to handle suspicious emails or calls could be the difference between protecting your assets or losing them.

### The "Who, What, When, and How" of Family Finances

So how do you avoid all this chaos? It starts with some good, old-fashioned communication. The who, what, when, and how of family finances can make sure everyone is rowing in the same direction and maybe even save you a few gray hairs in the process. Here's what everyone needs to know:

- **Who** is in charge of what? Does one person handle the day-to-day expenses while the other focuses on long-term investments? Is there someone overseeing the estate plan, defining everyone's role to ensure that nothing slips through the cracks?
- **What** are the family's financial goals? Are you saving for a child or grandchild's education? Planning for retirement? Wanting to go on a family trip? Everyone needs to know what the goals are so you don't end up with someone saving and someone else spending like a freewheeling Rockefeller.

- **When** will financial decisions be made? Set up regular check-ins—monthly, quarterly, yearly—whatever works. Regular financial discussions mean you'll keep everyone on track and catch problems before they snowball.
- **How** will the money be managed? Are you budgeting together? Are investments a group decision, or does one person take the lead? How you handle the money is just as important as what you're doing with it. Having clear guidelines avoids confusion and late-night panic over mysterious bank charges.

Let's face it—arguments about money aren't exactly rare in families. But you can avoid a lot of unnecessary drama by simply setting clear expectations. When everyone knows the family's financial game plan, there's less room for fights about overspending or unrealistic assumptions about who's paying for what.

Without clear communication, you might end up with siblings fighting over an inheritance simply because no one knew what the estate plan actually said. Or you might see parents struggling to cover their living expenses because their adult kids assumed retirement was already taken care of. Whatever the situation, talking it out ahead of time can prevent major headaches and more than a few awkward holiday dinners.

### Training Takeaway: Communication Is the Secret Ingredient

Keeping your family's finances on track isn't just about having a rock-solid financial plan—it's about *talking* about that plan. Regular, honest, and open communication can stop a lot of problems before they start. Whether it's protecting

MELISSA COX, CFP®

family members from scams, figuring out who's responsible for what, or making sure everyone knows the financial goals, talking about the "who, what, when, and how" of finances is crucial.

## Family Finances:
## Death—Literally the Final Chapter

Unfortunately, I've become all too familiar with the twists and turns that can come with settling an estate. While I guide families through this process as a CFP®, I always bring in an estate planning attorney to help us navigate the legal maze. Even the simplest cases can throw a curveball or two, so having an expert by your side is crucial.

I'm lucky to work with Dallas-based attorney Derek Christensen who helped me with this chapter to make sure it's not just informative but also practical for families dealing with the toughest of times.

Death is unavoidable. To put it bluntly, it just plain sucks. Losing someone you love is one of the most difficult experiences you'll ever face. It's a time of grief, reflection, and emotional upheaval, and the last thing you want to think about is finances.

Yet the reality is that life—and bills—keep moving forward, even when you feel like time should stop. This chapter is about giving you guidance to navigate the financial side of loss, step by step, with as much peace as possible.

### Preparing for Death: Anticipating the Inevitable

In some cases, death can be anticipated—whether it's due to a long-term illness, a coma, or end-of-life care such as hospice. While it's a difficult and emotional time, being proactive about financial matters can provide a sense of peace and control. If you find yourself in this situation, it's important to take steps to ensure your loved one's financial affairs are in order.

Your loved one comes first. But while you're focusing on what matters most, it's also important to avoid any financial surprises down the road. A little preparation now can save you a lot of headaches later.

The first thing to do is to revisit the financial planning binder. This is where all your preparation pays off. Review and update all assets and liabilities, making sure that everything is properly documented. Double-check whose names are on all accounts, property titles, and insurance policies, and make sure that beneficiary designations are current.

Double-check for the most recent estate plan; it's easy for old documents to slip through the cracks, but this is the last chance for an ex-spouse to make their big return if the will isn't up to date. No one wants that kind of surprise!

Getting this sorted in advance helps you avoid the scramble later and gives you a clear picture of what you're dealing with. Plus, it makes the probate process smoother, so you can spend more time focusing on family and less on paperwork.

### Timeline for Handling Financial Matters After Death

Grief doesn't follow a schedule, and neither should your financial decisions. In the immediate aftermath of losing someone, emotions can be overwhelming, making it hard to think clearly. That's why I always encourage people to avoid making any big, expensive decisions for at least six months to a year. This is not the time to sell the house, buy a new car, or make significant changes to your investments.

Focus on taking care of yourself and your loved ones. The only financial steps you should prioritize are those that are truly necessary—like managing ongoing bills, securing access to accounts, and handling any final expenses. Everything else can wait until you're in a more stable emotional place to make decisions with clarity, not from a place of grief.

However, there are certain tasks that need to be handled sooner rather than later to avoid complications or additional stress. Let's talk about a basic timeline to help you prioritize what needs to be done and when.

### Within the First Week

- Obtain Death Certificates. As grim as it sounds, you'll need multiple certified copies (10-15 is usually a good number) from your county records office. Death certificates are required by many institutions before they'll release or transfer assets, so it's best to have plenty on hand.
- Notify Social Security. If the deceased was receiving Social Security, let the agency know to stop payments. You might also be entitled to survivor benefits, so ask about that, too.
- Arrange for Immediate Bills to Be Paid. Life keeps moving, so make sure essentials like mortgage, utilities, and insurance premiums are paid to avoid any gaps in coverage or penalties.
- Contact Employer (if applicable). If the deceased was em-

ployed, notify their employer to stop wages, and inquire about any life insurance or retirement benefits.

## Within the First Month

- Notify Financial Institutions. Banks, investment firms, credit unions—contact them all. You'll need to present death certificates to start closing or transferring accounts.
- File for Life Insurance. If there was a life insurance policy, it's time to file the claim. This process usually requires the policy number and, you guessed it, another death certificate.
- Meet with a Probate Attorney (if necessary). If the estate is on the larger side or issues are getting complicated with disputes or multiple properties, now's the time to get a probate attorney involved. They can help navigate the legal side. (More on that below.)
- Notify Creditors and Close Credit Card Accounts. You don't want those credit card bills piling up. Notify creditors, close accounts that were solely in the deceased's name, and keep an eye on joint accounts.

## Within 3 Months

- Start the Probate Process. If the estate needs to go through probate, this is when you'll start. The executor, and if necessary, a probate attorney will handle the legal distribution of assets.
- Settle Debts. Work with the estate's executor to settle any outstanding debts. Remember, the estate is responsible for paying debts, not you personally—unless you're a co-signer on anything. When it comes to handling an estate's creditors, depending on your state's laws, you usually have two

options. You take the proactive step of notifying creditors that the individual has passed. Once notified, creditors have 4 months to bring a claim against the estate. While this shortens the timeline for resolving debts, it also makes it more likely that creditors will submit a claim. Or you can wait for creditors to reach out. The downside? You'll have to wait out the statute of limitations, which is 2 years in Texas for example, before waiving any outstanding debts. This decision depends on your circumstances and whether you'd prefer to close out debts quickly or play the waiting game. Consulting with a probate attorney can help you weigh your options and determine the best course of action for the estate.

**Within 6 Months to 1 Year:**

- Distribute Remaining Assets. Once probate is wrapped up, the remaining assets can be distributed to beneficiaries. However, before making any distributions, it's essential to double-check with an attorney to ensure everything is done correctly. This step is crucial to avoid misunderstandings or mistakes about who gets what or how assets should be divided. Misinterpreting the will or estate plan could lead to unintended consequences or legal complications, so it's always better to be safe and confirm with a professional before moving forward.

- File Final Tax Returns. You'll need to file the deceased's final federal and state tax returns. If the estate generated income after death, an estate tax return may also be required. Additionally, any applicable estate taxes must be paid within 9 months of the person's passing. This can be a complex process, so it's important to work with both an accountant and an attorney to ensure everything is filed correctly and any tax liabilities are addressed on time.

- Revisit Your Own Financial Plan. Now that the dust has settled, it's time to make any big adjustments to your own financial plan—whether that means updating your estate plan, changing investments, or reworking your insurance needs.

### When to Involve a Probate Attorney

You might be wondering, "Do I need a probate attorney for this?" Well, it depends. Probate is the legal process of validating the will and distributing assets, but it doesn't always require an attorney. If the estate is small and straightforward, you might be able to handle it without legal help. But there are times when an attorney is essential. Here are some signs that you'll likely need a probate attorney:

- **No Will Exists**. If there isn't a will, the estate will be divided according to state laws, so it's wise to get legal help to ensure everything is done properly.
- **Large or Complex Estate**. If the estate involves businesses, multiple properties, or complicated investments, a probate attorney will help manage it all.
- **Disputes Among Heirs**. If there's a fight brewing over who gets what, a probate attorney can mediate and ensure disagreements are handled legally.
- **Multiple State Properties**. If the deceased owned properties in more than one state, rules get a little trickier, and probate may need to be opened in each state.

When someone passes away without a will, they are said to have died *intestate,* and the state's laws of intestacy will determine how their estate is distributed. It's important to remember that intestacy laws are state-specific, so the rules for who gets what vary depending on where the person lived.

Believe it or not, even celebrities—who you'd think would have their estates in order—have fallen into this trap.

For example, Prince passed away in 2016 without a will, leaving behind an estate worth hundreds of millions of dollars. With no clear direction on how to divide his fortune, his heirs had to wait years for the court to settle the estate. His situation was a prime example of how not having a plan can turn into a lengthy and complicated legal battle.

Aretha Franklin, the Queen of Soul, also passed away without a formal will in 2018. Although handwritten documents were later found, her estate is still being sorted out in 2024 due to the lack of an official estate plan.

Actor Chadwick Boseman, best known for *Black Panther,* also passed away in 2020 without a will. His widow and parents have had to navigate the intestacy process in California, highlighting that even successful individuals often overlook estate planning.

## Intestacy

Intestacy occurs when a person dies without having left a valid will. In that case, the deceased's estate is handed over to probate courts to identify beneficiaries and allocate assets, according to state law.

These high-profile cases show that estate planning is essential, whether you have millions or not. Without a will, the division of assets may not reflect your wishes, leading to confusion, family conflict, and lengthy court proceedings.

For example, if the person who passed without a will was married with children, in many states, the surviving spouse and children will share the estate. In some states, the spouse might receive 50% of the estate, and the other half is split equally among the children. If there was no spouse, the estate is typically divided equally among the children. If a child has passed away but has their own descendants, that child's portion may pass to their kids. If the individual was married but had no children, the surviving spouse may inherit the entire estate. But in some states, the spouse may have to share it with the deceased's parents or siblings. If someone passes with no immediate family, the estate may pass to parents, siblings, or even more distant relatives like cousins.

If no relatives can be found, the estate could ultimately end up in the hands of the state itself. And in a blended family, intestacy laws can get even trickier when there are children from previous marriages. In these cases, the current spouse and children from prior relationships may end up sharing the estate, which can lead to unexpected splits.

In short, without a will, state laws decide—and you may not like what they decide! Making sure you have an estate plan in place is crucial to prevent surprises and ensure your wishes are honored.

### The Costs of Probate

The costs of hiring a probate attorney can vary, but they

generally range from $3,000 to $10,000 depending on the complexity of the estate. Some attorneys charge by the hour, while others may take a percentage of the estate's value, often around 3% to 5%. Keep this in mind when planning the settlement of the estate, as probate and attorney fees can reduce the amount ultimately passed on to the beneficiaries.

That said, probate expenses are reimbursed from the estate, even if you have to initially cover them out of pocket. This includes attorney fees, court fees, and any other costs associated with administering the estate. So while you may need to pay upfront, you'll be reimbursed once the estate is settled.

It's important to remember that state laws vary when it comes to probate. In some states, like Texas, there's an option to file a Small Estate Affidavit, which can be a simpler, faster way to handle smaller estates. This is generally used when the total value of the estate is under a certain threshold (in Texas, for example, it's $75,000) and can allow heirs to bypass formal probate altogether. The affidavit essentially states that the estate is small enough to be distributed without the need for a court-supervised process. It's a great option for uncomplicated estates where there's no significant debt or property involved.

However, not all states offer this option, and the rules about what qualifies as a "small estate" can vary. This is where a probate attorney can be invaluable—they'll help you navigate the specific laws in your state and determine the best approach for settling the estate.

### Gathering the Right Documents

Once you've caught your breath, you'll need to gather the right documents to start closing or transferring the deceased's accounts. And here's yet another time that the financial planning binder we talked about earlier comes in handy.

Documents you'll need include:

- **Death Certificates**. Hopefully you ordered at least 10-15 certified copies. You'll need these for just about everything.
- **Will and Testament**. If a will exists, this will be crucial for probate and guiding asset distribution.
- **Letters Testamentary**. If you're the executor, this legal document proves you have the authority to act on behalf of the estate.
- **Social Security Information**: You'll need the deceased's Social Security number to notify the SSA and apply for any survivor benefits.
- **Marriage Certificate**: If you're the spouse, you may need this document to access certain benefits or joint accounts.

*Training Takeaway:*
*Navigating Grief and Finances Together*

Grief is tough enough without the weight of financial responsibilities pressing down on you. The most important thing to remember is that you don't have to do everything at once. Take it step by step, and lean on professionals—financial advisors, probate attorneys, accountants—who can help you through the process. Take a deep breath, focus on what needs to be done today, and know that everything else will fall into place over time. There's no rush—just focus on what matters most: taking care of yourself and your family.

# The Long-Term Rewards
## of a Future-Focused Mindset

Although we are at the finish line of this book, you could be at the starting line of your personal financial journey. If there's one message I hope you've taken away from *Future-Focused Wealth* it's that your financial future is entirely within your control. Whether you're just getting started or refining a plan you've had in place for years, the important thing is that you're taking steps in the right direction—*your* direction, at *your* pace.

Throughout this book, we've covered the essentials of financial health: understanding money concepts, creating a comprehensive plan, embracing the power of compound growth, building generational wealth, and clearing the mental hurdles that often trip us up along the way. But here's the thing: None of these steps are one-time tasks. Financial planning is a lifelong journey, and like any journey, there will be moments when you need to course-correct. Life changes, and so do our goals, priorities, and challenges.

Hopefully by now you have noticed that I'm a big believer in the idea of *my race, my pace*. It's the philosophy that has helped me guide clients for many years, and it's the mindset I

MELISSA COX, CFP®

> True financial success doesn't come from shortcuts. It comes from building a strong foundation, staying focused on your long-term goals, and making steady progress—even if it's one small step at a time.

hope you'll carry forward with you. Your financial journey is uniquely yours. It doesn't matter if your neighbor retires at 50 or your best friend buys a second home. What matters is that you're working toward *your* goals at a pace that makes sense for *you*.

The financial world can feel overwhelming at times. There's always someone trying to sell you a "get-rich-quick" scheme or a magic-bullet investment that promises overnight wealth. But if there's one thing I've learned it's that true financial success doesn't come from shortcuts. It comes from building a strong foundation, staying focused on your long-term goals, and making steady progress—even if it's one small step at a time.

I've mentioned it before, but it's worth repeating: Your financial plan should be flexible. Life happens. Things change. You might need to adjust your goals, shift your budget, or rethink your investment strategy at some point. And that's okay! Flexibility is a strength in financial planning. It means you can adapt to life's surprises while still keeping your long-term goals in sight.

So if you hit a bump in the road (and we all do), don't panic. Take a step back, reassess, and adjust as needed. Whether it's a job loss, a medical emergency, or an unexpected opportunity, your plan is there to support you—not hold you back.

I know financial planning can sometimes feel like a marathon, especially when you're focused on long-term goals like retirement or building generational wealth. But don't forget to celebrate your wins along the way—no matter how small they might seem. Whether you paid off a credit card, hit a savings milestone, or simply created your first budget, take a moment to acknowledge your progress. Every step forward is worth celebrating.

And here's a secret: Those small wins add up. Before you know it, you'll look back and realize just how far you've come. The key is staying consistent, staying committed, and staying flexible as life unfolds.

The idea behind *Future-Focused Wealth* is simple: Planning for tomorrow gives you the freedom to live your life today. By taking control of your financial future, you're not only setting yourself up for success—you're also giving yourself peace of mind. You're building the flexibility to handle life's curveballs, the security to pursue your dreams, and the confidence to know you're on the right track.

And if you're thinking about the next generation, your financial decisions today can help ensure that your family is taken care of in the future. That's a powerful legacy to leave behind—one that reflects your hard work, your values, and your commitment to long-term success.

As you continue your financial journey, remember this: You've got everything you need to succeed. It doesn't matter where you're starting from or what obstacles you've faced in

MELISSA COX, CFP®

the past. What matters is that you're here taking control of your financial future and moving forward with a clear plan.

You don't have to be perfect, and you don't have to have everything figured out. So take a deep breath, keep your eyes on the road ahead, and trust that each step you take is getting you closer to the future you want. Yes, financial success is a marathon, not a sprint.

I'm rooting for you.

Here's to a future focused on your financial freedom—one that's filled with smart decisions, personal growth, and maybe even a little fun along the way. *You've got this!*

# Acknowledgments

To my mom, thank you for holding the door open for me to walk through life. Your love and belief in me have been the foundation of everything I've achieved.

To my family, thank you for supporting my dreams, no matter how big they've grown.

To my friends, thank you for keeping me sane through every twist and turn in the race of life.

To my mentor, Rick Fetterman, thank you for an incredible 20-year journey filled with guidance, insight, and the occasional well-placed nudge to keep me moving forward.

To my amazing clients, thank you for showing me the beauty and uniqueness in every financial plan—it's been a privilege to be part of your journeys.

And to Janis Dworkis and Christine Nicolette-Gonzalez, thank you for guiding me through this fun adventure and helping me develop a whole new wealth of talents I never knew I had.

This book is a reflection of all of you.

MELISSA COX, CFP®

# Glossary

**401(k):** A retirement savings plan offered by employers where employees can contribute pre-tax or Roth dollars, often with employer matching, to grow their savings through investments like stocks and bonds.

**403(a):** A retirement plan similar to a 401(k), often used by public sector employers, allowing pre-tax contributions to grow tax-deferred.

**403(b):** A retirement plan similar to a 401(k), specifically for employees of public schools, nonprofits, and certain tax-exempt organizations.

**529 Plan:** Tax-advantaged savings plans for education expenses.

**72(t) Distributions:** Refer to early withdrawals from an IRA or other qualified retirement plan taken before age 59½ without incurring the usual 10% early withdrawal penalty. These distributions must follow a specific schedule of substantially equal periodic payments (SEPP) over the account holder's life expectancy and adhere to IRS rules to avoid penalties.

**Above-the-Line Deductions:** Adjustments to income, such as IRA contributions or student loan interest, that reduce adjusted gross income without requiring itemization.

**Accelerated Death Benefit:** A life insurance feature allowing early payouts for terminally ill policyholders.

**Active Investing:** A hands-on investment strategy where individuals or fund managers buy and sell securities frequently, aiming to outperform the market.

**Adjusted Gross Income (AGI):** Total income minus certain deductions, serving as the basis for calculating taxable income.

**Allocation:** Refers to the process of dividing financial resources, such as money or investments, across different asset classes (e.g., stocks, bonds, cash) or categories to achieve a specific financial goal.

**Alpha:** A measure of an investment's ability to outperform a market benchmark, indicating the added value of an active management strategy.

**Alternative Investments:** Financial assets outside traditional categories like stocks, bonds, and cash. They include options like real estate, private equity, hedge funds, commodities, art, and cryptocurrencies. These investments are often less liquid and more complex but can provide diversification and potentially higher returns in a portfolio.

**Alternative Minimum Tax (AMT):** A parallel tax system ensuring high earners pay at least a minimum amount of tax, even with deductions and credits.

**Annuity:** An insurance product that provides regular income payments, often used for retirement, funded through either a lump sum or periodic contributions.

**Artificial Intelligence (AI):** The simulation of human intelligence in machines designed to perform tasks such as learning, problem-solving, decision-making, and language understanding. It uses algorithms and data to improve performance over time and is applied across various fields, including finance, healthcare, and technology.

**Asset Allocation:** The strategy of dividing investments among different asset categories (e.g., stocks, bonds, cash) to balance risk and reward based on financial goals and time horizons.

**Asset Classes:** Broad categories of investments, such as stocks, bonds, real estate, and cash, each with distinct risk and return characteristics.

**Below-the-Line Deductions:** Itemized deductions taken after adjusted gross income is calculated, such as mortgage interest or medical expenses exceeding a threshold.

**Benchmarking:** The process of comparing the performance of an investment, portfolio, or financial strategy against a standard index or metric, such as the S&P 500. It helps investors and professionals evaluate whether an investment is meeting, exceeding, or underperforming relative to market expectations.

**Beneficiary Designation:** Naming an individual or entity to receive assets like life insurance or retirement accounts upon your death.

**Beneficiary IRA:** An inherited retirement account that allows the beneficiary to maintain its tax-advantaged status while withdrawing funds according to specific rules, such as the 10-year rule for most non-spousal beneficiaries. Withdrawals are typically taxed as income if the original account was tax-deferred.

**Beta:** A measure of a stock's volatility compared to the overall market, indicating risk.

**Bonds:** Fixed-income investments where you lend money to a government or corporation in exchange for regular interest payments and the return of principal at maturity.

**Brokerage Account:** An investment account that allows individuals to buy and sell securities, such as stocks, bonds, and mutual funds.

**Broker-Dealer:** A financial institution or individual that buys and sells securities on behalf of clients (broker role) and for its own account (dealer role). Broker-dealers facilitate transactions, provide investment advice, and often play a critical role in the financial markets by maintaining liquidity and access to securities.

**Capital Gains:** The profit realized when an asset, like a stock or property, is sold for more than its purchase price.

**Capital Gains Tax:** A tax levied on the profit from the sale of investments, with rates depending on how long the asset was held and one's income.

**Catastrophic Insurance:** Low-cost health insurance covering high medical expenses after meeting a high deductible, ideal for rare but costly events.

**Catch-Up Contributions:** Additional contributions allowed for individuals aged 50 and older to boost retirement savings in accounts like 401(k)s and IRAs.

**Certified Financial Planner (CFP®):** A professional designation requiring education, experience, and ethics, focused on comprehensive financial planning.

**Certified Public Accountant (CPA):** A licensed professional specializing in accounting, taxation, and financial auditing. CPAs meet rigorous education, examination, and experience requirements and are authorized to represent clients before the IRS.

**Charitable Remainder Trust (CRT):** A tax-advantaged trust that provides income to the donor or other beneficiaries for a specified period, with the remaining assets donated to a designated charity. It allows donors to reduce estate taxes, receive an income stream, and support charitable causes.

**Child Tax Credit:** A tax credit for taxpayers with qualifying children under 17, reducing the amount of taxes owed.

**Compound Growth:** The process where investment earnings generate additional earnings over time, amplifying growth.

**Contributions:** The amounts of money deposited into a retirement account, such as an IRA or 401(k), typically subject to annual limits set by the IRS. Contributions may be pre-tax (traditional accounts) or after-tax (Roth accounts), affecting how the funds are taxed.

**Cost of Attendance (COA):** The total estimated cost of attending a college, including tuition, fees, room, board, books, and transportation.

**Coverdell Education Savings Account (ESA):** A tax-advantaged account for educational expenses.

**Cryptocurrency:** A digital currency that operates on blockchain technology, such as Bitcoin or Ethereum, known for its decentralized nature and price volatility.

**Custodian:** A financial institution or individual responsible for safeguarding a client's financial assets, such as stocks or bonds, ensuring they are held securely.

**Defined Benefit Plan:** A traditional pension plan guaranteeing a specific monthly payment in retirement, typically based on salary and years of service.

**Defined Contribution Plan:** A retirement plan, like a 401(k), where contributions are fixed, but the retirement benefit depends on investment performance.

**DINK (Dual Income, No Kids):** A household with two incomes and no dependents, often with higher disposable income.

**Disability Insurance:** Replaces part of your income if an illness or injury prevents you from working.

**Distributions:** Withdrawals taken from a retirement account, which may be subject to taxes and penalties depending on the account type and the age of the account holder. For traditional accounts, distributions are taxed as income, while Roth distributions are generally tax-free if certain conditions are met.

**Diversification:** The practice of spreading investments across different assets, industries, or regions to reduce risk.

**Dividend:** A share of a company's profits distributed to shareholders, often as cash payments or additional stock.

**Dollar-Cost Averaging (DCA):** An investment strategy where an investor regularly invests money into a particular asset, regardless of its price or market conditions. By spreading purchases over time, the investor creates an average cost per share.

**Dollar-Weighted Return:** A method of calculating investment performance that accounts for cash flows in and out of the portfolio.

**Donor-Advised Fund (DAF):** A charitable giving account that allows donors to make contributions, receive an immediate tax deduction, and recommend grants to their favorite charities over time. It provides flexibility in philanthropic planning while simplifying the process of managing donations.

**Dual Enrollment:** Earning college credits while still in high school to save on future tuition.

**Early Action:** A non-binding college application process where students apply early, typically by November, and receive a college decision sooner but are not obligated to attend if accepted. This option allows students to compare offers and financial aid packages from multiple schools before making a decision.

**Early Decision:** A binding college application process where students apply to their first-choice school early, typically by November, and are contractually bound to attend if accepted. Students must withdraw all other applications upon acceptance, making this option ideal for those who are certain about their top choice and have the money to pay for it.

**Enrolled Agent (EA):** A federally licensed tax professional authorized to represent taxpayers before the IRS. EAs specialize in tax preparation, planning, and resolution, earning their designation through passing a comprehensive IRS exam or having prior IRS experience.

**Errors and Omissions (E&O) Policy:** A type of professional liability insurance that protects individuals and businesses from claims of negligence, mistakes, or failure to deliver promised services. It covers legal costs and settlements, ensuring professionals like financial advisors, real estate agents, and consultants are safeguarded against costly lawsuits.

**ESG Investing (Environmental, Social, and Governance):** An investment approach that considers a company's performance and impact in areas like environmental sustainability, social responsibility, and ethical governance. It aims to align financial goals with values while potentially mitigating risks related to non-financial factors.

**Estate:** The total sum of a person's assets, debts, and property to be distributed after their death.

**Estate Planner/Estate Planning Attorney:** A professional specializing in creating legal and financial strategies to manage an individual's estate during their lifetime and upon their death.

**Estate Tax:** A tax levied on the transfer of an estate's value to heirs after the owner's death.

**Exchange-Traded Funds (ETFs):** Investment funds traded on stock exchanges that hold a diversified portfolio of assets, combining the benefits of mutual funds and stocks.

**Expected Family Contribution (EFC) / Student Aid Index (SAI):** A calculation used to determine a family's ability to pay for college.

**Expense Ratio:** The percentage of a fund's assets used for administrative and management expenses.

**FAFSA (Free Application for Federal Student Aid):** The primary form to determine eligibility for financial aid.

**Family Office Advisor:** A professional or firm that provides holistic financial management and planning services exclusively for wealthy families.

**FDIC Limit:** Refers to the maximum amount of coverage provided by the Federal Deposit Insurance Corporation (FDIC) for deposits held in insured banks. Currently, the FDIC insures up to $250,000 per depositor, per bank, per account ownership category, protecting funds in checking, savings, money market accounts, and CDs against bank failures.

**Federal Student Loans:** Government-backed loans for students, often with lower interest rates and flexible repayment options.

**Fiduciary:** A person or entity legally and ethically obligated to act in the best interests of another party, such as a client or beneficiary. This duty requires loyalty, transparency, and avoiding conflicts of interest, ensuring decisions prioritize the interests of those they serve above their own.

**Financial Advisor:** A professional offering guidance on investments, retirement, taxes, and estate planning.

**Financial Analyst:** A professional who evaluates financial data and market trends to assist businesses and individuals in making investment decisions.

**Financial Coach:** A professional who helps clients develop healthy money habits and achieve financial goals through education, guidance, and accountability. Unlike financial advisors, coaches focus on foundational skills like budgeting, saving, and debt management rather than on investment or wealth-building strategies.

**Flexible Spending Account (FSA):** An employer-sponsored, tax-advantaged account that lets employees save pre-tax dollars for eligible healthcare or dependent care expenses. Funds are typically "use it or lose it" within the plan year, though some plans allow limited carryovers or grace periods.

**Futures Contract:** A legal agreement to buy or sell a specific asset at a predetermined price on a set future date. Commonly used for hedging or speculative purposes, it obligates both parties to fulfill the terms of the contract, regardless of market conditions at the time of settlement.

**Generation-Skipping Trust:** A trust that transfers wealth to grandchildren, bypassing the children, often for tax-saving purposes.

**Gift Tax:** A tax on transfers of money or property above a certain annual limit that exceeds the lifetime exemption.

**Grants:** Need-based financial aid that does not need to be repaid.

**Gross Income:** The total income earned by an individual or entity before any deductions, taxes, or expenses are applied. It includes wages, salaries, business revenue, investment income, and other sources of earnings.

**Growth Investing:** An investment strategy focused on buying stocks or assets expected to grow faster than the overall market.

**Health Savings Account (HSA):** A tax-advantaged account for medical expenses available to those with high-deductible health plans; unused funds roll over and can be invested.

**Hedge Funds:** Private investment funds that use advanced strategies, like leverage and short selling, to generate high returns, often accessible only to accredited investors.

**HENRY (High Earner, Not Rich Yet):** Individuals with high incomes but limited wealth due to lifestyle expenses or career stage

**High Deductible Health Plan (HDHP):** A health insurance plan with lower premiums but higher deductibles compared to traditional plans. Often paired with Health Savings Accounts (HSAs), it is designed to encourage consumers to manage healthcare expenses more actively.

**High-Yield Savings Account:** A type of savings account that offers a significantly higher interest rate than traditional savings accounts. These accounts, often offered by online banks, are ideal for earning more on short-term savings while maintaining easy access to funds.

**HMO (Health Maintenance Organization):** Health insurance requiring members to use in-network providers for care.

**Homeowner's Insurance:** Protects your home and belongings against damage, theft, and liability for injuries on your property.

**Index Funds**: A type of mutual fund or ETF designed to replicate the performance of a specific market index, such as the S&P 500.

**Indexed Universal Life (IUL):** A type of permanent life insurance that combines a death benefit with a cash value component tied to the performance of a stock market index, such as the S&P 500. It offers flexible premiums, potential for cash value growth, and downside protection through guaranteed minimum interest rates.

**Intestacy:** Refers to the legal situation that arises when a person dies without a valid will, leaving their estate to be distributed according to state laws. These laws determine the heirs and the proportion of assets they receive, often prioritizing close relatives.

**Intestate:** Dying without a valid will, leaving asset distribution to be determined by state laws.

**IRA (Individual Retirement Account):** A tax-advantaged account for retirement savings, with options for tax-deductible contributions (Traditional IRA) or tax-free withdrawals (Roth IRA).

**Irrevocable Life Insurance Trust (ILIT):** A trust specifically designed to own a life insurance policy and manage its proceeds. By removing the policy from the grantor's estate, an ILIT helps reduce estate taxes, protect the insurance proceeds from creditors, and ensure controlled distribution to beneficiaries according to the trust's terms.

**Irrevocable Trust:** A trust that cannot be changed or canceled without the permission of the beneficiaries.

**Keogh Plan:** A retirement plan for self-employed individuals and small businesses offering tax-deferred contributions and growth.

**Kiddie Tax:** A federal tax rule that applies to unearned income (e.g., investment income) of children under 18, or full-time students under 24, whose income exceeds a certain threshold. This income is taxed at the parents' marginal tax rate to prevent families from shifting investment income to children in lower tax brackets to reduce their overall tax liability.

**Liquidity:** The ease with which an asset can be converted to cash without significantly affecting its price.

**Living Will:** A legal document outlining your preferences for medical care if you become incapacitated and unable to communicate.

**Long-Term Care Insurance:** Covers expenses for nursing homes, assisted living, or in-home care, reducing the financial burden of extended care needs.

**Marginal Tax Rate:** The percentage of tax paid on your last dollar of taxable income, reflecting your highest tax bracket.

**Market Capitalization:** The total value of a company's outstanding shares of stock, calculated by multiplying the current stock price by the number of shares outstanding. It is commonly used to measure a company's size and overall market value.

**Medical Directives:** Documents that specify your healthcare wishes and appoint a decision-maker if you're unable to communicate.

**Merit-Based Aid:** Scholarships and grants awarded based on academic, athletic, or artistic achievements.

**Money Market:** Refers to a segment of the financial market where short-term, low-risk debt instruments are traded. Examples include Treasury bills, certificates of deposit (CDs), and commercial paper. Money market accounts and mutual funds allow investors to earn interest while maintaining liquidity and stability.

**Money Market Fund:** A type of mutual fund that invests in low-risk, short-term debt securities such as Treasury bills, commercial paper, and certificates of deposit (CDs). Designed for stability and liquidity, money market funds aim to provide a safe place for investors to park cash while earning a modest return.

**Mutual Funds:** Pooled investments managed by professionals that allow investors to buy into a diversified portfolio of stocks, bonds, or other securities.

**Need-Based Aid:** Financial aid awarded based on a family's financial situation.

**Net Income:** The amount of income remaining after all deductions, taxes, and expenses have been subtracted from gross income. It represents the actual earnings available for saving, spending, or reinvestment.

**Non-Qualified Account:** A standard investment or savings account that does not receive special tax benefits. Examples include brokerage accounts and savings accounts where contributions are made with after-tax dollars, and earnings may be taxed annually.

**Parent PLUS Loans:** Federal loans available to parents to help cover their child's educational costs.

**Passive Investing:** An investment strategy focused on tracking market indices and minimizing trading to achieve steady, long-term returns.

**Pension Plan:** A retirement benefit program funded by an employer, where employees receive a predetermined, regular income after retiring. The benefit amount is typically based on factors such as years of service, salary history, and age, with the employer managing the investments and bearing the risk.

**Permanent Life Insurance:** Life insurance that lasts one's entire life and often includes a cash value component.

**PPO (Preferred Provider Organization):** Health insurance offering more flexibility to see in- and out-of-network doctors at differing costs.

**Power of Attorney:** Legal authorization for someone to act on your behalf in financial or medical matters if you're incapacitated.

**Preferred Stocks:** Shares of a company that have a fixed dividend and priority over common stock in asset distribution but usually lack voting rights.

**Premium:** The amount you pay for an insurance policy, typically monthly or annually.

**Prepaid Tuition Plans:** Plans allowing families to pay today's tuition rates for future education.

**Private Student Loans:** Non-federal loans provided by private lenders for education expenses.

**Probate:** The legal process of validating a will and settling an estate, including paying debts and distributing assets to heirs.

**Qualified Account:** A retirement account that receives special tax advantages under IRS rules, such as tax-deferred growth or tax-free withdrawals. Examples include 401(k)s, Traditional IRAs, and Roth IRAs.

**Qualified Charitable Distributions (QCD):** Tax-free donations made directly from an IRA as distributions to a charity, often counting toward RMDs.

**Rate of Return:** The gain or loss of an investment over time, expressed as a percentage of the initial amount invested.

**Rebalancing:** The process of adjusting the allocation of assets in a portfolio to match the original or desired target allocation.

**Registered Investment Advisor (RIA):** A firm or individual providing investment advice and legally required to act in a fiduciary capacity.

**REITs (Real Estate Investment Trusts):** Companies that own or finance income-producing real estate, allowing investors to earn returns without owning property directly.

**Renter's Insurance:** Covers personal belongings in a rental property and liability for injuries to others in your home.

**Required Minimum Distribution (RMD):** The minimum amount that must be withdrawn annually from certain retirement accounts, such as traditional IRAs and 401(k)s, once the account holder reaches a specified age. The withdrawals are mandated by the IRS to ensure taxes are paid on pre-tax contributions and earnings.

**Revocable Trust:** A trust that can be altered or terminated by the grantor during their lifetime.

**Rider:** An optional add-on to an insurance or annuity policy that provides additional benefits or coverage for specific situations, often at an extra cost. Examples include a waiver of premium rider for disability or a long-term care rider on a life insurance policy.

**Robo-Advisors:** Automated platforms that use algorithms to manage investment portfolios based on individual goals and risk tolerance.

**Rollover IRA:** An IRA created by transferring funds from a workplace retirement plan, like a 401(k), to maintain tax-deferred growth.

**Roth 401(k):** A workplace retirement account funded with after-tax dollars, allowing tax-free withdrawals in retirement.

**Roth Conversion:** Involves transferring funds from a tax-deferred retirement account, like a traditional IRA, to a Roth IRA. While the converted amount is subject to income tax at the time of the transfer, future withdrawals from the Roth IRA, including earnings, are tax-free if certain conditions are met.

**Roth IRA:** A retirement account funded with after-tax dollars, where investments grow tax-free, and withdrawals are tax-free in retirement.

**Rule of 7s:** A financial principle stating that, at an average annual return of 10%, an investment will approximately double every 7 years due to the power of compound growth. This concept highlights the importance of starting early and staying consistent to maximize long-term wealth accumulation.

**Scholarships:** Financial awards that do not need to be repaid, based on merit, need, or other criteria.

**Self-Insurance:** Setting aside funds to cover potential risks instead of purchasing insurance.

**SEP IRA (Simplified Employee Pension):** A retirement account for self-employed individuals or small businesses with higher contribution limits than traditional IRAs.

**Sharpe Ratio:** A metric evaluating the risk-adjusted return of an investment, higher values indicating better risk-reward efficiency.

**Simple IRA:** A retirement plan for small businesses allowing employees and employers to contribute, with lower administrative costs than a 401(k).

**SIPC Insurance:** Protection provided by the Securities Investor Protection Corporation (SIPC) for investors against the loss of securities or cash held in a brokerage account due to the brokerage firm's failure. Coverage is up to $500,000 per account, including a $250,000 limit for cash, but it does not protect against investment losses due to market fluctuations.

**Split-Dollar Insurance**: A life insurance arrangement between two parties (e.g., employer and employee) sharing costs and benefits.

**Spousal IRA:** An Individual Retirement Account that allows a working spouse to contribute to a retirement account for a non-working or low-earning spouse. Contributions follow the same limits and tax rules as regular IRAs, enabling couples to maximize their combined retirement savings.

**Standard Deduction:** A fixed dollar amount reducing taxable income, with amounts based on filing status (e.g., single or married).

**Step-Up in Basis:** An adjustment of an inherited asset's value to its market value at the time of the original owner's death, reducing capital gains tax.

**Stocks:** Shares of ownership in a company, entitling shareholders to a portion of profits and often to voting rights.

**Student Loan Interest Deduction:** A tax deduction for interest paid on student loans.

**Systemic Risk:** The risk of a widespread failure in the financial system, often triggered by the collapse of a major institution or market segment.

**Tax-Loss Harvesting:** An investment strategy where an investor sells securities at a loss to offset taxable gains from other investments. This approach can reduce an investor's overall tax liability while allowing reinvestment in similar assets to maintain portfolio objectives.

**Ten-Year Rule:** A rule for inherited IRAs requiring beneficiaries to withdraw all funds within ten years of the original owner's death.

**Term Life Insurance:** Life insurance covering a set period, such as 20 or 30 years, without cash value accumulation.

**"The Line":** These words on a tax return typically refer to the point where Adjusted Gross Income (AGI) is calculated. It separates income from deductions and determines eligibility for many tax credits and deductions, making it a crucial figure in tax planning and filing.

**TIPS (Treasury Inflation-Protected Securities):** U.S. Treasury bonds indexed to inflation, protecting investors from the decline in purchasing power over time.

**Traditional IRA:** A retirement account where contributions may be tax-deductible, but withdrawals in retirement are taxed as ordinary income.

**Treasury Bonds:** Long-term, low-risk debt securities issued by the U.S. government to fund public projects and operations.

**Trust:** A legal arrangement in which a trustee manages assets on behalf of beneficiaries according to the trust's terms.

**Trustee:** The individual or institution responsible for managing assets held in a trust.

**Umbrella Policy:** Extra liability coverage protecting against large claims that exceed standard home or auto policies.

**Universal Life Insurance:** Flexible permanent life insurance allowing adjustments to premiums and death benefits.

**Value Investing:** An investment strategy focused on finding undervalued stocks believed to be trading below their intrinsic value.

**Volatility:** The degree of variation in the price of an asset over time, often used as a measure of market risk.

**Whole Life Insurance:** Permanent life insurance with fixed premiums and guaranteed cash value accumulation.

**Will:** A legal document specifying how a person's assets should be distributed upon their death.

**Work-Study Programs:** Federally funded programs that provide part-time jobs for students with financial need.

Melissa Cox is a Certified Financial Planner™ with over 20 years experience guiding individuals and families toward financial clarity and security. Having worked with clients at every stage of life—from young professionals just starting out to retirees planning their legacy—Melissa is passionate about making financial planning approachable, actionable, and empowering. With a relatable approach and a deep commitment to financial literacy, she breaks down complex financial concepts into practical steps anyone can follow. Through education and strategic planning, she empowers individuals to make informed decisions that align with their values and long-term goals, decisions that lead to freedom in future-focused wealth.

Beyond her role as a financial planner and author, Melissa is a devoted mother who is passionate about showing her daughters how to successfully balance work and home life—at her own pace—while still being a #BossMom. She leads by example, proving that building a successful career doesn't mean sacrificing family time, and that true wealth isn't just financial—it's about creating a fulfilling, purpose-driven life.

When she's not advising clients or writing, Melissa enjoys traveling, cheering on her favorite sports teams, and making memories with her family.